PEACE, WAR
AND THE YOUNG CATHOLIC

PEACE, WAR AND THE YOUNG CATHOLIC

by JOHN B. SHEERIN
of the PAULIST FATHERS

PAULIST PRESS
New York / Paramus / Toronto

Library of Congress
Catalog Card Number: 72-91458

ISBN 0-8091-1733-9

Published by Paulist Press
Editorial Office: 1865 Broadway, N.Y., N.Y. 10023
Business Office: 400 Sette Drive, Paramus, N.J. 07652

Printed and bound in the
United States of America

To

Thomas More

a man for this season

Contents

I
The Reality
of War

At the center of life there are invisible forces that conspire to make life worth living. An unseen power in the earth causes flowers to break through the ground in springtime. An intangible force in the heart of the musician breaks through wooden or metal instruments to produce music that seems to lift the soul to another level of life. Poetry sheds a warm wonder and a bright glory over our prosaic human existence. These are forces that hallow our lives, blessing our days with joy.

There are other forces, however, that work against life: disease, famine, plague and war. The first three are often beyond human control. War is different. Men start wars. There is nothing in nature itself that brings on wars. National leaders initiate wars and combat soldiers are carefully taught how to handle death-dealing weapons. War is an intruder into the natural rhythms of life. It is the ghastly skeleton at the feast.

Unfortunately most of us find it hard to appreciate the serenity of peace unless we have tasted the pain and bitterness of war. Soldiers on both sides in our American Civil War never appreciated peace until the miseries of war caused them to huddle around

1

campfires singing and yearning for "the dawn of peace." In World War II most Britishers had to endure "blood, toil, tears and sweat" before they came to realize how wonderful it would be when "the lights go on again all over the world." The young clerk from middle America appreciated peace after he saw his buddies killed in the guerrilla warfare in Vietnam.

It is unfortunate that so many learn peace only through war. For it is possible to learn the agony of war without having to undergo it. Just as it is possible to discover the nature of fire without walking into the flames. Through a study of war we can learn to love peace, to love it enough to work unsparingly for peace, to keep before our minds a blessed vision of peace. The Second Vatican Council says: "Divine Providence urgently demands of us that we free ourselves from the age-old slavery of war." By studying war we can help to break the ancient curse for ourselves and for the whole human family.

What is war? Without going into endless ramifications and fine distinctions we can describe war as a conflict between or among nations in which each army attempts to kill as many enemies as possible. No one in his right mind would attempt today to approve of war as a venture good in itself. General Sherman's remark that "war is hell" is endorsed by military men as an accurate description of what has been happening on battlefields ever since the beginning of armed conflicts. Even military experts support war only as an evil that is necessary under certain circumstances. War is a messy business but unfortunately we cannot expect it to disappear overnight from this planetary spaceship on which we are all passengers. The first

World War was fought by Americans "to end all wars" but twenty years later the second World War broke out in mechanical butchery such as the world had never known.

No, war is far from obsolete. It is still an instrument of national policy, as the political scientists note. The day may come when cannons will be seen only in museums, as Victor Hugo hoped, but that day is not close at hand. Peacemakers are blessed, as the Beatitudes say, but they have a long, hard pull up a rocky road before they can outlaw war forever. The goal of world peace, however, is well worth a lifetime of dedicated effort. Pope Paul's words to the United Nations, "No more war, war never again," are a challenge to us to work for peace. While we strive for total abolition of war, we can at least hope to bring about a reduction in the number of wars and a letup in its savagery. This means hard work.

It means that peacemakers have to study, analyze and scrutinize the arguments advanced by those who support war. They have to read up on the factors that are said to conduce to war. The peacemaker has no magic wand that dispels all confusion and doubt and solves all problems relating to peace. He has to work hard in studying peace if he hopes to prove his case by a fair preponderance of the evidence, as the lawyers say. Enthusiasm for the cause of peace is, of course, necessary but knowledge of the facts about the morality and humaneness of war is also imperative. As followers of Jesus Christ, the kindest and gentlest member of our race, we can do nothing nobler than to work for peace on earth.

While it is true that war itself is far from obsolete at

present, it is also true that the old notion of war as a *glorious adventure* is gradually becoming obsolete. You who work for peace can hasten its demise. Centuries ago, men in the prime of life often succumbed to the music of a marching military band or the glamor of a uniform, rushing to join the service in a state of euphoria. Not so today, thank God. We are coming to realize that war is a tragedy more than flesh and blood can bear, a brawl in which we engage—if we must— only with utmost reluctance and only after the solemn assurance of our national leaders that they have done everything humanly possible to avoid the conflict.

The Prussian field marshal Von Moltke, in 1850, claimed that war is a glorious element in God's government of the world. "It develops in man the noblest virtues—courage and self-denial, love of duty and self-sacrifice. Without it the world sinks into materialism." This sounds incredible and yet it was the philosophy of many great warriors of the 19th century. This soap-opera romanticizing of war was not peculiar to Prussians. There was a time in our own American history when some of our leaders actually thought of war as a heavenly blessing for inferior nations. Our own Theodore Roosevelt once eulogized war as a beneficent force that could bring progress and civilization to backward nations. In 1896 he wrote: "It is indeed a warped, perverse and silly morality which would forbid a course of conquest that has turned whole continents into the seats of mighty and flourishing civilized nations" (*Winning of the West*, Theodore Roosevelt, 1896). Probably he had been reading British authors of the time who maintained that Britain had a divine mission to bring culture and civilization to her colonies. Unquestionably Britain did **confer** some benefits on backward peoples but most of her former colonies are not grateful today for blessings imposed on them at the point of a gun.

At the turn of the century our American forebears probably read Roosevelt's words with solemn attention, if not approval. Today they sound like nonsense. Such rhetoric smacks of "the gunboat diplomacy" that disgraced American history at times in the past. To attempt to justify our international escapades in pious rhetoric only heightens our "imperialism." Certainly young people today would snicker at such efforts to glorify war and armed interventions. They are not cynical, just realistic and honest.

The Anatomy of War

What is war really like? I refer, of course, to modern war, not to the Wars of the Roses, the American Revolution or the Boxer Rebellion. In examining the morality of war, there is no point in discussing the uncomplicated and non-technical conflicts of the past. The focus is war as it is fought today and as it will probably be fought in the immediate future.

Since 1945 there have been many minor wars in underdeveloped countries. Some have been called *guerrilla wars* (*guerrilla* meaning a little war) and the rebels in these wars are now referred to as *guerrillas*. Usually these little wars began when the native peasants rose up in a revolution against their French, British, Portuguese or Belgian rulers in countries of Asia, Africa or Latin America. In Mao Tse Tung's phrase, "The guerrilla is the fish, the peasant is the water in which he swims." That is, the armed guerrillas are as helpless without the aid of the neighboring peasants as a fish is out of water. The peasants provide the fighters with food, supplies and information about the enemy.

The Vietnam war was at the outset a war of rebellion. After the Vietnamese drove out the Japanese and then the French, it looked as though all Vietnam would enjoy peace and national unity. But peasants in the southern part of Vietnam rose up against the Diem regime, and eventually were aided by the Vietnamese from the North who were Communists as well as patriotic Vietnamese.

When the American ground troops arrived in Vietnam, therefore, they had to fight Vietnamese guerrillas who had long years of experience in jungle warfare. There were no front lines, no trenches such as the young soldier had read about in accounts of World War I and World War II. Nor was this fighting a replica of the Korean battles. The Vietnamese guerrillas were seldom visible. They were waiting for the young American footsoldier but they were hiding in ambush for him in the tall grass of the jungle. His ears were assaulted by the sound of sniper fire, exploding bombs and grenades. When he saw a peasant in the fields, he was not sure whether he was friend or Vietcong terrorist. The most innocent-looking child might be carrying a grenade cleverly concealed. The American stepped gingerly along the jungle paths for fear of detonating a mine or booby trap. Nor was it any picnic to walk miles in wet boots through endless puddles left by the monsoons, to wear a helmet, to carry a rucksack weighing twice as much as himself. All this to the tune of bullets and mortars and B-40s popping around him.

At times he felt frustrated, mad, desperate. He saw

buddies die under a hail of bullets but he could see no enemy. He was tempted to be cynical and skeptical about the war, infuriated at the deserters and draft evaders and yet wondering, why am I here? Was he helping these Orientals to shake off the Communists? Were they worth dying for? Was he fighting the Vietcong only to keep a tin-pan dictator in his job at Saigon? Psychologically he was confused, bewildered. In his better moments he contented himself perhaps with the thought that he had a messy job to do, that he would do it to the best of his ability and live to tell the folks about this Donnybrook. When depressed, however, he would sometimes nurse a grudge against the South Vietnamese soldiers as lazy or chickenhearted or perhaps he would pan all "gooks," all slant-eyed people, all "dinks."

That he felt depressed at times was understandable. The ordinary combat-infantryman, or "grunt" as he was often called, had a tough job. He worked long hours driving a truck or loading helicopters, marching, marching, marching or standing guard at night. No wonder he bewailed his lot. He was exhausted. He usually respected his immediate officers but damned the big-shots in Washington, the press, the anti-war demonstrators at home. No wonder he fell into black moods. The "grunt" was too fundamentally good to enjoy burning down hamlets and depriving civilians of their homes and ancestral relics, too decent to enjoy herding refugees into barbed-wire camps.

If one of his best friends was killed next to him, he probably felt a desperate urge to take revenge. His instinct was to shoot anything or anybody in sight: it would give him some relief to know he had killed an enemy and so he would let loose at anything that moved. Sometimes it was little children that moved! This was war as it appeared to the ordinary footsoldier in Vietnam.

What strikes us about the war on the ground was the primitive conditions in which the footsoldier had to fight. What impresses us about the war in the air was the highly developed technology of the weapons. The war in Vietnam has given us a preview of the highly sophisticated type of warfare that will take place in the skies during the ghastly future—unless the world regains its sanity.

General William Westmoreland spoke of "the automated battlefield." This is an apt description of the war as fought in Vietnam by Americans with electronic weapons on the ground and in the air. The air war especially brought out a dazzling variety of eagle-eyed electronic instruments. One of the electronic systems employed was called "The Air Support System." It relied on little instruments called *sensors* that were flung into the ground by high-speed aircraft and blended with the foliage. These *sensors* were mechanisms that detected the faintest sounds in the vicinity. Small radio microphones were also dropped to the ground by tiny parachutes. These sensors and microphones picked up whispered conversations among Vietnamese peasants or soldiers as well as tell-tale sounds of movement or any slight noise that might indicate the presence of human persons.

The mechanisms relayed the sounds to American planes flying high above the area and the pilots in turn relayed the sounds to a ground control station in nearby Thailand. At the ground control station there, computers got to work, determining whether or not to give the order for an air strike at the sounds. If the decision was *Yes,* the computers transmitted the order to aircraft on the ground in Thailand or on an airplane carrier attached to the 7th Fleet. The aircraft then took off from the carrier or home base, was directed to the target, then dropped bombs on signal from computerized instruments in the plane.

The second system was called "The Ground Tactical System." It depended on helicopter gunships, laser-guided and electronically-guided bombs and partially on "The Air Support System" for ultimate control of the bombs. Both these systems are extremely complex but they have this in common—they are designed to kill. Their destructive capacity is increased by dropping canisters containing thousands of tiny bomblets which can burst open to inflict severe injury on contact. Some of these anti-personnel weapons have alluring names. The *Dragontooth* looks like a nail clipper: the *Cluster Bomb Unit* contains tiny Guava bomblets with their thousands of pellets: the *Gravel Mine* is the size and shape of a teabag.

This type of war resembles a nineteenth-century war about as much as a spaceship resembles an ox-cart. It is also totally different from other twentieth-century wars. When General Zhukov began his all-out offensive against the Germans at the end of World War II, he gave the signal for the turning on of searchlights to illuminate the German positions. Then came the artillery barrage and the Russian troops began moving toward the German positions. Soon German flak and anti-tank guns began to pour their deadly fire into Zhukov's men, blowing infantrymen off tanks and setting fire to armored vehicles. The Russians fell back but only temporarily. Eventually, by sheer force of numbers, the Russians smashed the

German defenses and moved forward. Within two weeks the Russians triumphantly raised the Soviet flag over the Reichstag in Berlin.

What made the American air war in Vietnam, Laos and Cambodia radically different from the Soviet-Nazi war? It was the *impersonal* character of the American air war. The pilot of the B-52 bomber could not see the enemy face to face. He saw blips on the radar screen. He saw no signs of life ordinarily and yet he was using weapons that could cause more death and destruction than a hundred rifles or hand grenades.

One pilot, testifying before a Government Committee, said: "Most of the pilots just go along and figure, well it's a job. And that's the way we all looked at it. You fly. You see flak at night. That's about as close to war as we get. Sometimes you get shot down but you don't see any of the explosions. You can look back and see 'em but you don't see any of the blood or any of the flesh. It's a very clean and impersonal war." (Jon Floyd in *Congressional Record,* April 6-7, 1971)

In other wars, the soldier on the battlefield saw the enemy. The very sight of him bleeding or writhing in agony often induced a certain measure of pity or sympathy for the afflicted man. This was true especially if the enemy cried for mercy, for the average soldier felt a certain amount of horror and digust at the thought of murdering a man. True, in other wars fighting men found that they could kill without having second thoughts about it if they were firing at an enemy some distance away and could not see his face. The bomber pilot can see no human face, no sign of a human form. He kills mechanically, sight unseen.

The huge number of casualties resulting from bombing raids also seems to dull the sense of pity and sympathy in the men who drop the bombs. By a curious psychological quirk, a man who slaughters an enormous number of human beings usually has fewer scruples about it than the man who kills only one or two. The vast numbers of Jewish victims in the Nazi camps probably dulled their executioners' sensitivities. The Jewish victims became mere statistics rather than persons. Sometimes casualties are not even statistics to bomber pilots. They simply press the button or lever without knowing how many they kill.

Why would a normal American take part in what he knows might be a mass murder of civilians? Because it does not look like murder to him. Iver Peterson, aboard the U.S. Coral Sea, a carrier in the South China Sea, attempted to describe what went on in the mind of pilots who flew their bombers from this floating air base toward targets on the Ho Chi Minh Trail or the mainland in North Vietnam (*New York Times,* January 9, 1972, p. 1). Pilots told Petersen that they were not concerned about fine points of national policy but simply wanted to do the work for which they had been trained. It was for them a dangerous and exacting profession but a fascinating one. "Whatever our feelings about the war," said Lieutenant Mendenhall, a bombardier-navigator, "we're still out there and we're still dropping our bombs—and we enjoy it." Or as Lieutenant Merril York said: "We fly because we like it. It's exciting but challenging and that's what we're trained to do." Another pilot said, "I think history will show that we should never have been over here . . . but we're doing a damn good job of the dirty job we've got to do."

In May, 1972 the U.S. Air Force began to use new types of weapons said to have been phenomenally successful in bombing North Vietnam targets with astounding accuracy. Some are guided by laser beams, some by television. Called "smart bombs", they are reputed to hit targets cleanly without destroying buildings or killing civilians in the vicinity. If the reports about the accuracy of these weapons are true, then it will be possible for pilots to be "discriminating" in their bombing of big cities. Some military officials say that the work being done with laser beams is as important as the project that produced the atomic bomb in World War II. The Air Force has also disclosed plans for a dream plane of the future, a TV-eyed robot bomber flown from miles away by a pilot using radio controls. The development of weapons such as these conjures up some startling possibilities. For instance, what will happen if laser beams are used with nuclear bombs?

The Odor of War

No one today praises war as an instrument of national policy. It has no odor of sanctity about it. Most national leaders admit quite frankly that it is a noxious and undesirable way of settling international quarrels, and they explain that they would gladly refrain from war if they could get redress for their grievances in some other way. In fact, many modern wars have started out with eloquent expressions of regret and reluctance on the part of the aggressor. These apologies however usually reflect no sincere regret but a keen awareness of the fact that war has a bad odor and is unpopular with the general public.

The relevant question, however, is not whether statesmen are reluctant to use force but whether they will use force if they don't get what they want by peaceful means. Many statesmen, unfortunately, rank peace rather low on the totem pole of national priorities. And sad to say this is quite as true of the younger nations as of the older states. If underdeveloped nations in the Third World, just emerging from colonialism, do not get what they want, they are just as quick to start a war as were the old imperialistic war lords.

Even the United States, with a solid reputation for being a peace-loving nation, has at times belied its own reputation. Robert Osgood and Robert Tucker in their scholarly *Force, Order and Justice* note that Adlai Stevenson, at the time of India's grab of Goa in December, 1961, told the U.N. Security Council that the U.S. was protesting the incursion just as it had opposed such actions in the past whether committed by friend or foe. Yet, just a few months earlier, in April, 1961, the U.S. had organized and supported an armed intervention in Cuba. On that occasion President Kennedy had announced that it was contrary to American tradition to engage in attacks on other countries but he wanted it clearly understood that the U.S. Government would not hesitate in meeting its primary obligation, "the security of our nation."

A Practical Criterion of War?

The hard-headed realist says that the only relevant question in regard to a war is: can it succeed? (It reminds us of the professional bank robber who says the only relevant question about a bank robbery is: did the robber get away with the loot?) Some political experts say that war or the threat of war is the only practical way for a nation to get what it wants. In fact, some claim that the threat of force is gradually becoming the weapon of the future because public opinion is becoming more and more influential in making policy and public opinion is impressed only by force or the threat of force. This, of course, is sheer speculation. No one can know how public opinion will react to force or threats. Frequently in the past enemy threats of force only stiffened the public's resistance to hostile acts.

It has been said that war can never succeed in killing an idea. That is, that a nation may capture territory by force of arms but cannot force the conquered people to abandon the basic idea underlying their cause. Osgood and Tucker claim that this is false and that victorious nations have been known to destroy an enemy's dominant ideas as well as defeat its army: witness the World War II destruction of Nazism. The Nazi army was the standard bearer of the Nazi idea. However, Fascism was the basic idea behind Nazism and Fascism is not altogether dead yet. Communists conquered the occupied countries in Eastern Europe but they did not destroy the Christian faith in the minds and hearts of the Poles. They are still staunchly Catholic. Likewise, the United States might defeat the Soviet military forces but could we kill Communism? I don't think so. The Roman Empire suppressed Christianity for a few centuries but the fiercest persecutions only strengthened the faith of the Christians. "The blood of martyrs is the seed of Christians." Force never decides anything except the victory of the moment. God is not always on the side of the winner and truth is not always with the unbeatable army.

II
Conscience

Shall I take part in war? This is a question that is vividly and painfully relevant to the young man called to military service when war breaks out. It is also a question that deserves an answer from any man or woman who takes part in the organized war effort. If a particular war is just, the young man can participate in it in defense of his country against unjust aggression. If it is unjust, he must not bear arms. For he is committing murder if he kills in an unjust war. The problem facing other citizens, whether men or women, is not as immediate and impelling as the problem confronting the man of draft age as they will probably not be called upon to kill. Yet they also must make a decision. If the war is just, they can take part in the general war effort. If unjust, they should shun it as evil.

The decision is a very personal affair. No man or woman of integrity can delegate the making of the decision to another person. Not his Government. Not his father or mother. Not his parish priest. These may help him make him up his mind but they cannot decide for him. For it is he alone who will be putting himself possibly into a situation in which he may commit murder. The American Bishops described the personal nature of this responsibility in their 1966 Pastoral Letter: "While we cannot resolve all the issues

15

involved in the Vietnam conflict, it is clearly our duty to insist that they be kept under constant moral scrutiny. No one is free to evade his responsibility by leaving it entirely to others to make moral judgments." (Nov. 17, 1966)

Conscience is a profoundly respected word today. Thirty years ago, it was often used in a derogatory sense to discredit the rigor of the Puritan conscience, especially in matters of sex. In the 1960s however it became an "in" word. During those years torrents of literature came from the presses dealing with the rights of conscientious objectors. The civil rights movement also focused on conscience, asking the American public to follow their consciences in the matter of equal opportunity for blacks, Puerto Ricans and Mexicans as well as the white majority. The man or woman of conscience is honest. Such a person judges impartially, weighs facts and opinions without prejudice, acts responsibly. There is nothing false about him, no facade, no posturing, no double-dealing or chicanery. In this the conscientious person reflects the younger generation's respect for the virtue of honesty.

Yet there does seem to be a considerable amount of confusion about conscience. So much so that certain theologians are quite reluctant to offer a definition of conscience. I think we are safe, however, in starting from the premise that conscience exists only in a person. It is a person making judgments. The person is helped by God but it is the person who makes the judgment. At least in Christian thinking there is no concept of a lonely soul making a conscientious judgment all by himself in lonely splendor. Rather, the person in some remote and mysterious way experiences the presence of God in making the judgment and freely follows or rejects His inspiration. It was said very aptly at the Second Vatican Council that the human person achieves the peak of human activity when he responds to God speaking to him in conscience. He can do nothing nobler or better than this.

This may seem a bit pious and churchy. Actually it is not. Even American law grants exemption to religious conscientious objectors because American law presumes that God speaks to the religious conscience. God wants each of us to become the fully human person He intended us to become. To help us become fully-developed persons and to help the whole human family become more human, He communicates His grace to us. We know from Scripture that He is specially interested in promoting peace throughout the world. So He speaks to us in conscience to keep us working as peacemakers to transform the world.

Conscience is not a part of the person any more than it is a mystic voice or a light that flashes red or green. We used to say that conscience is *reason* judging the rightness or wrongness of an act. This definition did not leave much room for the heart and the emotions in the making of a conscientious judgment. Today we are understandably dubious about praising the *head* and neglecting the *heart*. The extraordinary genius of physicists has produced the frightful death-dealing weapons used in war but they should have had the *heart* to control the use of these weapons. Head and heart must work in unison. The nuclear bomb could be used to blast out sources of water in deserts to make the deserts blossom like the rose but highly intelligent scientists and policy planners allowed the bomb to be used at Hiroshima to kill men, women and children.

Conscience is head and heart working together. It is the human person loving intensely and thinking carefully, forever searching for the truth, the whole truth and nothing but the truth. This means that the conscientious peacemaker will try to get all possible help and advice from other persons before making up his mind about a war.

You who are peacemakers will naturally ask men and women you respect for their judgment on a particular war. You will, of course, hear discordant opinions: some will be based on snap-judgments, some on big-name experts or so-called authoritative sources. You will weigh these opinions, making allowance for the fact this man is temperamentally a liberal, that man a conservative. So be it. As race track fans say, "Difference of opinion makes horse races." In arriving at a decision, don't expect to come to a conclusion that is all black or all white. It will be grey. The arrogant and dogmatic person imagines he is infallible and comes to absolute, unquestionable conclusions, then condemns all who disagree with him as incarnate devils. The humble person is content to have conclusions that are eminently reasonable.

In this inner experience, the person encounters Christ who challenges him or her to make a decision. It is not ordinarily an experience in feeling but in faith. We do not feel His presence as we would experience the presence of a neighbor. When we are presented with a question as serious as that of participating in a war, Jesus sets up a conflict within us, something like God's call to Moses to set his people free. Moses hemmed and hawed and gave excuses why he should not go. He said he was not a leader, he could not be sure the people would listen to him—and all that sort of thing. But God kept after him while this struggle was going on and finally Moses capitulated. He decided to take God's advice and he set forth on his journey to set his people free.

I think it is important to keep in mind that it is Jesus Himself within us, and that obedience to conscience is obedience to Him. The Christian is ultimately responsible not to any human person but to God alone. To follow Him may be a rough ordeal but we can be sure we are going in the right direction because He has no designs on us but truth and love.

In ordinary discussions of conscience we often hear some weird notions expressed, varying all the way from conscience as a lawcourt in which the judge has a nasty disposition to conscience as a policeman whose only job is to suppress sexual thoughts. One of the best statements of the Catholic concept of conscience is found in Vatican II's *Declaration on Religious Freedom*. That document stresses the personal nature of conscience. One adheres to the truth, says the *Declaration*, only by his own personal assent in conscience. No one has any right to impose his beliefs on anyone else: this would be tampering with conscience. The document says that it is by conscience that a man perceives divine truth and divine commands. "In all his activity he is bound to follow his conscience faithfully in order that he may come to God, the end and purpose of his life. It follows that he is not to be forced to act in a manner contrary to his conscience. Nor is he to be restrained from acting in accordance with his conscience, especially in religious matters."

Therefore, no person can force a man or woman to

act against his or her conscience. Every man must educate his conscience but having done so, he must follow it and his salvation is assured as long as he obeys conscience. Probably the most striking illustration of this primacy of conscience can be found in Cardinal Newman's reply to Prime Minister Gladstone who claimed that a Catholic could not be a good citizen because he had to obey the Pope at all costs and in every circumstance: "Hence it is never lawful to go against our conscience . . . I will drink to the Pope, if you please, still—to conscience first and to the Pope afterwards" (*A Letter Addressed to His Grace the Duke of Norfolk*).

Conflict with Loyalty to Government

It is obvious therefore that conscience must be given priority over any government. The conscientious person will try to be a good servant of his country and will faithfully observe its laws but if it comes to a conflict between his conscience and the state, he will follow conscience. The state exists for man, not man for the state. The Catholic teaching is that man was made for eternal life with God whereas the state exists to provide those conditions of life that will enable him to attain his goal. But if the government prevents a man from following his conscience, it is acting beyond the scope of the powers given to it by the people. Hence our Constitution says, "Congress shall make no law respecting an establishment of religion or prohibiting the free exercise thereof."

St. Thomas More, the man for all seasons, was perhaps the finest example of a man who paid due reverence and obedience to his government and yet to his conscience as well. He was no revolutionary. He gave to Caesar what was due to Caesar, to God what was God's but when there was a conflict, he made clear that God came first. He was a scholar and respected scholarship. He never made any snap judgments nor did he ever condemn the consciences of other men. Cranmer felt that More's failure to condemn the consciences of other men was an indication that More felt unsure of his own judgments. But the fact was that when statesmen or scholars expressed their opinions, More respected them but in a showdown he always put conscience above king or scholar. The difference between More and the sycophants around the King's throne was that they merely obeyed the laws of the state but he looked beyond to an ultimate standard of right and wrong that transcended any human code of law.

Thomas More rated the government of his time much higher than we would rate any government today. In fact, some English historians say he conceded too much to the state. This only serves to show the anguish in his conscience when he was trying to make up his mind about obeying the King by taking an oath that would violate his conscience. Robert W. Chambers quotes Plato as saying about the duty of following conscience: "Wherefore our battle is immortal, and the gods and the angels fight on our side, and we are their possessions . . ." More's glory is that he put every talent of mind and heart into the battle in his conscience and came to the conclusion that he was the King's good servant but God's first. He was one of history's greatest conscientious objectors.

Conflict with Loyalty to Family

As conscience takes priority over the civil authority so also it takes priority (after infancy) over the claims of the family. Called upon to take part in a war, some men are tempted to go along with the military tradition of their family. This can be a tremendously powerful influence in some cases. But conscience here has priority as in the case of the conflict between conscience and the state. "He who loves father or mother more than me is not worthy of me," said Jesus (Matthew 10, 34). Faced with a call to arms, some men have taken the easy way out if there was a family tradition of fighting in their country's wars. It is praiseworthy for a young man to ask his father's advice and opinion but his father cannot make the decision for him. Nor can the son say, "My father knows more about this than I do. I will keep peace in the family by going along with his verdict." It is not the father who may have to commit a murder if the war is unjust. It is the young man himself who may have to drop the bomb or shoot the rifle and he alone bears the ultimate responsibility. The whole Mystical Body may pray for him but he alone will have to stand before the Great Judge.

Alan Geyer, when editor of *Christian Century*, declared in a talk that a conscientious decision often involves a conflict of loyalties. He said that Protestant teaching lays a heavy stress on family loyalty, sometimes so much so as to idolize family life. The result, according to Geyer, is that young Protestants often find themselves caught between loyalty to family and loyalty to the cause of world peace. Following conscience becomes for the young Protestant a great interior struggle. Young Catholics have also undergone the same anguish of conscience. In some families, certain members have been superpatriots. The one absolute and ultimate loyalty, however, is to God. All else is secondary. "For God and country" is excellent theology provided we don't reverse the order of words.

III
The Christian Attitude
Toward War

It would certainly solve a lot of problems if God would answer our questions about war by giving us special revelations. I don't doubt that religious fanatics who started holy wars probably imagined they had special instructions from the Lord but ordinary mortals have to use their brains to arrive at the right answers. I have heard rabble rousers at peace rallies who gave the impression they had mystical radars on which they could read God's will about war. They were short on facts but long on moral indignation and denounced anyone who disagreed with them as walking devils. Most of us, however, know we have no direct pipeline to God, that we need God's grace even though we don't get private revelations. So we read and study everything we can get our hands on in search of clues to the proper Christian attitude toward war.

Naturally we start with the Bible. We want to see what the inspired writers who did receive revelations have said about war. Unfortunately the Scriptures are not very helpful because they are not very explicit. The Old Testament in places seems to deplore wars but in other places it exalts warriors as heroes of the religion of the One True God. Several texts say that Israel cannot be saved by weapons but by faith in

God or that war is a judgment on Israel. But there are other texts that show God as leading the army, delivering the enemy into the hands of the Jews or sending panic into the ranks of the enemy. The best we can say is that the texts dealing with war generally reflect the thought of those centuries about war. The holy war notion was common in the thinking of most nations. Father John McKenzie says that the Israelite concept of the holy war was a primitive type of morality but doubtfully more primitive than the modern concept of war.

Nor is the New Testament very helpful. Frequently you find similes and metaphors that seem to take war for granted as a fact of life. Occasionally you find texts that have been interpreted as indicating an opposition to war, such as "They that take the sword shall perish by the sword" (Matthew 26, 52). On the other hand, you will come across texts that seem to say just the opposite: "But now, let him who has a purse take it and likewise a wallet and let him who has no sword sell his tunic and buy one" (Luke 22, 36). A number of centurions are mentioned in the New Testament and cited as good men; in fact the centurion at Capernaum is specially commended by Jesus for his faith. Some readers have interpreted these texts as praise of the military profession, an interpretation that seems unwarranted.

Many Christians find a condemnation of war not in Scripture texts dealing with war but in texts dealing with the commandment of brotherly love. Jesus said that love of God and love of neighbor are the greatest of the commandments, and he made clear that everyone is the neighbor. The parable of the Good Samaritan brought this out vividly. To the Jews the

Samaritans were foreigners and heretics but the parable illustrated the fact that the Christian should love Jews and Samaritans, friends and enemies, the virtuous and the sinners. What might be called the charter of Christian charity is the unforgettable text in Matthew: "You have learnt how it was said: You must love your neighbor and hate your enemy. But I say this to you: love your enemies and pray for those who persecute you; in this way you will be sons of your Father in heaven, for he causes his sun to rise on bad men as well as good, and his rain to fall on honest and dishonest men alike. For if you love those who love you, what right have you to claim any credit? Even the tax collectors do as much, do they not? And if you save your greetings for your brothers, are you doing anything exceptional? Even the pagans do as much, do they not?" (Matthew 6, 43-48).

To reconcile war with this command of brotherly love would be quite a juggling act but supporters of war have often put a heavy emphasis on a text from St. Paul to prove that a Christian must obey his government when it enacts a draft law. In Romans 13, 1-2 St. Paul says: "You must all obey the governing authorities. Since all government comes from God, the civil authorities were appointed by God, and so anyone who resists authority is rebelling against God's decision, and such an act is bound to be punished."

I remember a Peace Mobilization in Washington in 1968. Bill Coffin, the Yale chaplain, was preaching on draft resistance in a Presbyterian church when the noted fundamentalist cleric, Rev. Carl McIntire, moved into the sanctuary. He demanded the right to rebut Dr. Coffin, which permission Coffin granted even though McIntire was "disastrously out of order." The fundamentalist leader then quoted the above text from St. Paul claiming that it clearly forbids any American Christian to disobey his government by resisting the draft. Bill Coffin responded by pointing out that St. Paul was presuming that the government was not commanding a violation of conscience. Then he drew a laugh from the audience by asking Rev. McIntire to explain why St. Paul was "in and out of jail so often." He followed this remark by quoting the words of St. Peter, "We must obey God rather than men."

When we read the New Testament, the Jesus that comes through the pages to us is a gentle, compassionate person but there are Christians who see a different Jesus in the incident in which he drove the moneychangers out of the Temple. They magnify the incident to prove that such a man of violence would never condemn war. In fact, there are Christians today who claim that Jesus was a revolutionary agitator. This, of course, is absurd. He never carried weapons as did the rebels of the day. They were ardent nationalists who wanted to overthrow the Roman Government but Jesus was friendly even with the tax collectors who collected taxes for the Government the revolutionaries hated. In short, there is no text in the New Testament to support the notion that Jesus was given to violence or linked to political insurrection.

The history of the early Church discloses no explicit proof that the Christians of the first four centuries were pro-war or anti-war. Personally I believe they were pacifists but this cannot be proved from their writings or from their recorded history. Unquestionably they refused to become soldiers, and if Roman soldiers were converted to the faith they were expected to give up the military profession. But we do not know what the reason was why they stayed away from joining the army. Some historians say that Christians in the first century expected the world to come to an end any moment, and that they felt they had more urgent business on their hands than joining the army. Other historians say that the early Christians avoided any collaboration with the pagan Government, especially any participation in the act of pagan worship that was required of recruits at the time of their induction into the army. Still other historians claim that Christians stayed away from the military profession simply because they felt they had something better to contribute to society than living in barracks and shooting an occasional rebel.

The fact is undeniable however that they did not join the army. Justin Martyr (2nd century) said that Christians no longer wage war on their enemies but have turned their swords into ploughshares. He was paraphrasing the prophecy of Isaiah of the Old Testament who looked forward to an age of peace: " . . . and they shall beat their swords into ploughshares and their spears into pruning hooks: nation shall not lift sword against nation, neither shall they learn war any more" (Isaiah 2, 4). These words from Isaiah are cut into stone in a building facing the United Nations building in New York.

The whole life style of the early Christians, however, was radically changed when Constantine was converted to Christianity and established the Christian religion as the official religion of the Empire in the 4th century. There is an old political maxim, "If you can't beat them, join them." Constantine's conversion was probably genuine but he saw he could not beat the Christians and so he joined them and enlisted Christianity in the service of the Empire. The hardy group of "subversives" now became conformists. Whereas the earlier Christians had felt that fighting wars was none of their business, now church leaders began to say that national defense was a duty of all citizens.

Yet it does seem that the Church was never really at ease in the new situation. Even in wars that churchmen considered just wars, Christians who killed the enemy had to do penance for shedding blood, and in many places the Church forbade priests to carry arms. Some bishops managed to make a convenient adjustment, ruling that killing in war was a sin but that penance could be assigned according to the number killed. Apparently some bishops permitted their people to participate in wars simply because they could not find it explicitly forbidden by Scripture. St. Augustine wrote: "Do not believe that anyone who deals with military weapons cannot please God. Holy David, who was such a great witness for God, served in this capacity: most of the people of that time were also in military service. . . . (John the Baptist) did not forbid them to serve under arms and John (the Baptist) exhorted them to be satisfied with their pay" (*Ep. 189,* no. 4; *PL* 33, 855). St. Thomas Aquinas did not condemn military service but said it was inappropriate to the religious vocation.

Since Scripture and Church History had no clear and uniform stand on the subject of war, mediaeval scholars tried to find out if human reason could fill in the void. They examined the fifth commandment, "Thou shalt not kill," but found it vague and general.

It seemed to them to forbid even the killing of an unjust aggressor. It did not seem to them quite right that a mother could not defend her child with maximum force against a madman threatening to kill the child. So the mediaeval scholars began to look at the question from the angle of natural rights. They elaborated the concept that every person has a right to use whatever force is necessary to repel an unjust aggressor. From that they went on to conclude that a city or nation, likewise, has a right to defend itself against unjust aggressors in order to assure citizens the opportunity of peaceful self-development and the general welfare of the community.

Roman Catholic teaching has followed rather closely this natural law line of thinking. Not all Christians do so, however. Many Protestants hold that the only criterion of moral conduct for Christians is the Bible and that the Christian can find the answers to questions about peace and war in the general biblical teaching on love of neighbor. Certain Protestant theologians feel that pagans can follow human reason as a moral guide but that Christians should follow the higher law of divine revelation. To which certain Catholics might respond, "Fine . . . but what are you going to do if you find the Bible teaching too vague and general?"

The contemporary Catholic teaching on war is, therefore, to a large degree the work of Catholic theologians using human reason under the inspirations of the Holy Spirit. That they have had the best of intentions is unquestioned; whether they have succeeded in shedding much light on a very complex question is a matter we shall examine in this book. The awful truth however is that most Christians, Catholic or Protestant, have paid little attention to Scripture, Church

History or human reason when the bugle sounded for war in recent centuries.

National patriotism as we know it did not exist in the Middle Ages. At that time all Europe was generally united in a common culture and religious faith (though there were feudal lords here and there who showed their independence occasionally by starting wars). But the nation-state as we know it today did not develop until the Reformation. From this time on, it was taken for granted that the ruler of a particular country or region determined the religion of the area. If you lived in a Protestant country you had to be loyal to the Protestant ruler. If you lived in a Catholic country you were the subject of the Catholic ruler. The unfortunate result was that national patriotism became a mixture of loyalty to a religion and loyalty to the state. Many wars became religious wars. Soldiers fought with fanatical fervor, believing that God was on their side against the heretics on the other side.

The Catholic bishops were closely tied to their government: the Protestant church leaders were tied to their Protestant-oriented government. These were unhappy and unfortunate marriages: the official Church in each case hesitated to question its government's decision to start a war. Moreover, both the Catholic and the Protestant clergy felt bound by St. Paul's words about the sin of resisting the civil authorities. Thus the Christian churches grew into the habit of cooperating with the government as soon as it began to launch a war. They helped the war effort, no questions asked. The ancient Hebrew prophets believed it was their business to condemn and denounce national leaders who perpetrated injustice: they were the public conscience. Too often the Christian church leaders approved unjust wars or at least kept their silence. So we had the strange spectacle of Christians fighting Christians with the blessing of their spiritual guides.

During the twentieth century, Christians have taken part in national wars with remarkable fervor. Usually they took it for granted that fighting for their country was a patriotic duty of the utmost urgency. In many cases they injected into the war hysteria a note of "holy anger," regarding pacifists as "godless foes" of the fatherland. Here in the United States, patriotism was often taught in Catholic schools as a virtue inlaid with special Catholic nuances, and Catholics are generally believed to have joined the armed services during this century in numbers well beyond their proportion of the population.

Certain sociologists claim that there was an historical reason why American Catholics cherished patriotism so highly. Many Catholics who came to America were immigrants who had been persecuted for their faith abroad. Arriving here, they fell in love with the American Republic and its tradition of freedom for all people as well as the economic opportunities the new world opened up for immigrants. What a contrast to the oppressive society that had discriminated against them in their homeland! They encountered bigots, of course, but they felt that the government was their friend and that they could share with Protestants and Jews the equal protection of American law.

Nevertheless these Catholic immigrants were painfully aware of the presence of the bigots and their insistence that Catholics could not make good American citizens. The bigots claimed that Catholics had a double loyalty—to the Pope as well as to the President—and that if it came to a showdown, the Catholics would give their loyalty to the Pope, as commanded by their religion. According to some sociologists, the result was that immigrant Catholics bent over backward to prove their loyalty and patriotism, especially when the President called young men to arms in time of war. This patriotism, say the sociologists, became an American Catholic tradition that at times amounted to superpatriotism.

The early Christians were in a somewhat parallel situation. They were suspected by the Gentile non-Christians of being deficient in civic virtue. So St. Peter told his followers to be on their good behavior "in case they speak against you as wrongdoers." Then he went on to ask his Christians to be loyal to the Emperor and to governors "for it is God's will that by doing right you should put to silence the ignorance of foolish men" (1 Peter 3, 13). But he did not suggest that they participate in wars.

American Catholics played a very important role in the first World War, which America entered in 1917. Like most Americans, they felt sure that the war against Germany was altogether just and right. Today there are political experts who condemn this war against Germany as grossly unjust but we must remember, in all fairness to our Catholic predecessors, that they formed their consciences on the basis of what they knew in 1917. Fifty-five years later, we are not quite so sure the war was just. We have learned that our government subjected its citizens to a barrage of false propaganda portraying the Germans as inhuman monsters, barbaric Huns. It's easy for us now to say that these Catholics should not have helped along an unjust war but we have no right to condemn their consciences. It is their glory that they followed their consciences. As a child I remember hearing the ghastly horror-tales about the hellish Huns. It never entered my mind that a government department would manufacture such stories. And I remember hearing that this was "a war to end all wars" and then running into the streets with my classmates to sell war bonds and stamps with the zeal of a crusader.

Again, American Catholics played a large role in the second World War. In contrast to World War I, the 1941-45 war is even now considered a just war by many of our best historians except that they condemn certain atrocious acts committed by Americans, such as the indiscriminate bombing of Dresden. The bombing of Dresden, as of Hiroshima and Nagasaki, reminds us of the stern condemnation of such bombing raids contained in a Vatican II document: "Any act of war aimed indiscriminately at the destruction of entire cities or of extensive areas along with their population is a crime against God and man himself. It merits unequivocal and unhesitating condemnation" (*Constitution on the Church in the Modern World*, n. 80). Do single acts of war such as the bombing of Dresden render an entire war immoral? A good question—but I fear it needs more attention than I can give it in this short chapter.

Most American Catholics supported the American involvement in Korea in the 1950s. It seemed to them a clear case of a just war of collective defense against unjust aggression. The U.N. Army, representing the peace-loving nations of the world, went to the defense of South Korea and most Americans were proud that the U.S. had a share in the peace-keeping police action of the U.N. Army. There were some Catholic conscientious objectors but they were relatively few.

At the outset of the American involvement in Vietnam, American Catholics generally gave their support to the enterprise. Possibly the fact that a Catholic president, John F. Kennedy, had initiated the move and the fact that Catholic refugees from the North had "voted with their feet" against Communism in the North —these facts undoubtedly entered into the Catholic reaction as the involvement continued. Nor should we neglect the fact that we were in those early years aiding the Catholic Diem. When the war escalated under President Johnson, however, a few Catholics began to protest—notably the Berrigan brothers—but most Catholics still supported the war. The American Bishops took no vigorous stand until November, 1971 when they declared that withdrawal from Vietnam was "a moral imperative of the highest priority." In their statement they condemned any further American involvement in these words: "At this point in history it seems clear to us that whatever good we hope to achieve through continued involvement in this war is now outweighed by the destruction of human life and of moral values which it inflicts." This was a reference to one of the most important conditions of the Just War theory, which will be discussed in the next chapter.

IV
The Just War Theory: A Test for Judging Wars

Total pacifists have no need of any moral criterion for judging the rightness or wrongness, the morality or immorality of particular wars. They regard all wars as immoral and unjust. Most Christians, however, are not total pacifists and believe that a just war is theoretically possible, however difficult it may be to conceive of a just war in reality today. Admittedly, the Just War theory has many shortcomings as a test of the morality of a war. The very title is objectionable to some persons. They say the words "just war" tend to imply that many wars are just and thus to lend respectability to an ugly phenomenon that is distasteful to civilized men and women.

It is true that war is distinctly unpopular today and the general impression is that the great majority of wars are and have been unjust. Unfortunately war seems to become popular in certain nations as soon as the war hysteria breaks out, and even responsible citizens begin to imagine that *this* particular war is a glaring exception to the general rule that wars are immoral. I must confess that there is the danger now as always that some Christians will abuse the Just War theory. In Europe, German Catholics have been known to interpret its conditions so as to justify wars started by Germany: French Catholics have interpreted the theory to justify French wars. So be it. Every good thing can be and has been abused: sex, the beauty of women, alcohol, nuclear energy.

Some Catholic writers, however, take the position that Pope John and Vatican II scrapped the Just War theory by saying that no war can be justified today. Pope John was apparently referring to nuclear wars when he wrote in *Pacem in Terris* that it is irrational in "this atomic age" to believe that war is still "an apt means of vindicating violated rights." But Vatican II stated clearly that a nation has a right to engage in a war of self-defense if there is no competent and sufficiently powerful authority at the international level to settle the quarrel.

As Dr. Ralph Potter of Harvard has pointed out, many church leaders after World War I became enthralled with a vision of peace and decided they would agree to nothing less than the abolition of all wars. They spurned the Just War theory as a tricky device that might be used to justify wars. As a result, says Potter, they became intellectually incapable of making a discriminating judgment on the morality or immorality of wars. Their assumption since World War II seems to have been that all modern wars will necessarily be nuclear wars. It is true that nuclear wars cannot be just but the critics of the Just War theory are wrong in thinking all modern wars must be nuclear wars. We have had a number of non-nuclear wars since 1945, some of them guerrilla wars, and it seems to me that the Just War theory can be applied to non-nuclear wars.

Yes, the Just War theory has its imperfections but I do not see any substitute for it in determining whether a war is moral or immoral. We have no litmus-paper test for wars, no mechanism to register degrees of morality. The Just War theory is the best test we have. I have often heard critics condemn it only to find them judging a war in different words but in concepts identical with those of the Just War theory.

The Just War theory has a long history. As I have already mentioned, Christians did not take part in wars before the time of Constantine. Therefore, they had no need to concern themselves in those early years about the rightness or wrongness of wars. But the situation changed with Constantine. Under the Christian Emperor, Christians were expected to fight wars. Now they were faced with a tough problem. How could a Christian reconcile the killing of his neighbor in war with Christ's commandment to love the neighbor, even love the neighbor who is an enemy? St. Augustine looked into the problem in the fifth century. He discovered that great minds like Plato and Aristotle had laid down certain principles regarding a just war, and so Augustine formed these principles into a criterion by which to judge a war as just or unjust. It was however no easy task for him to fit war into Christian teaching. Much as he admired these brilliant pagans, he found the whole problem baffling to him as a Christian. For he saw very clearly that no Christian could take a life since he could not value his life above that of his neighbor. He consoled the conscience, however, by deciding that peace is such a good thing that a Christian ruler, under certain conditions, could wage a war in order to restore or preserve peace. His Just War theory was not intended as a guide for ordinary citizens. It was to be a guide for Christian kings. The power to launch a war at that time resided in the king, not in the people.

During the intervening centuries, the Just War theory has been studied, analyzed and enunciated in many variant versions but the basic conditions are these:

1. The ruler must make a formal declaration of war.
2. The ruler must have a just cause for war.
3. The ruler must have a right intention.
4. The ruler must have reasonable grounds for believing that the good to be achieved by the war will outweigh the evils that will result from it.
5. The ruler must wage the war in accordance with natural and international law.
6. The ruler must try by every possible means to arbitrate the quarrel before starting the war.

(The *ruler* is the person or legislative body designated by law in a particular country as having authority to declare war. The American Constitution—Article 1, Section 8—states that Congress has the power to declare war.)

At first glance we might feel that these conditions are too intellectual. War inevitably stirs up violent emotions pro or con: are we expected to judge a war the way we might judge a problem in higher mathematics? No, war does stir up emotions but we ought to have our emotions under control when we judge a war. In the past too many men let their emotions run away with them as soon as they heard the bugle call. To make a right judgment we must be able to take a calm, cool look at the whole war situation in all its details.

The first condition required for a just war is that the proper authority must make a formal declaration of war. During the Vietnam war, anti-war critics claimed that American involvement in the war was illegal because Congress had never declared war against North Vietnam, Congress alone having authority to declare war. The Constitution gives this power to Congress along with the power to raise and support armies. (Article II, Section 2 describes the President as commander in chief of the armed forces, having emergency powers when needed for national defense.)

Congress did pass the Tonkin Gulf Resolution in 1964 empowering President Johnson to bomb the mainland of Vietnam and some supporters of the war said that this resolution was "a moral equivalent" of a declaration of war. Congress, however, annulled this resolution in 1972 so that it could no longer be considered an authorization of war. Whereupon Congress deliberated on bills that would reaffirm the war powers of Congress without hampering the President in times of threats to national security.

I fear that too much attention has been given in the past to this need of a formal declaration of war. Probably certain citizens imagined that a war was right and proper just because it had been declared. But a declared war is not moral simply because it has been formally declared. Murder is murder whether publicly proclaimed or kept secret. Said a pirate to a Roman ruler: "You loot a country and call it official policy. I loot property and you call it piracy."

The second condition is that the ruler must have a just cause. Most Christian experts agree that the only just cause today is defense against unjust aggression. The only possible just war is a defensive war. In peacetime one citizen may attack another only in self-defense. A nation, likewise, may attack another nation only in self-defense or in defense of a nation unjustly attacked. Therefore, no nation can declare war in order to punish another nation or to protect the foreign investments of its citizens or to maintain a balance of power or to preserve its culture. Charity demands that we come to the aid of a neighbor who is being attacked and charity demands that we aid a neighbor nation that is unjustly attacked. This right to help another is as sacred as a nation's right to defend itself. However, we should not too quickly approve an intervention without scrutinizing it carefully. What looks like a foreign invasion to us may actually be a civil war in another country, and we should not get involved in other countries' civil wars. Let other nations take care of their own domestic affairs. We Americans resented Soviet Russia's interference in Hungary's civil war in 1956, and Lincoln warned European nations to stay out of our Civil War.

Vatican II conceded that a nation has a right to wage a war in order to defend itself against unjust aggression. "As long as the danger of war remains and there is no competent and sufficiently powerful authority at the international level, governments cannot be denied the right to legitimate defense once every means of peaceful settlement has been exhausted" (*Constitution on the Church in the Modern World*, n. 79). In the context to this sentence, the document notes that it is "one thing to undertake military action for the just defense of the people and something else again to seek the subjugation of other nations."

In a radio address (December 24, 1944) Pope

Pius XII spoke of the urgent need to ban all wars of aggression. He said that such wars are a shameful blot on the history of mankind. In another address (October 19, 1953) the Pope asserted that launching a war as a school of heroic virtue can be called "madness." He made it very obvious (October 3, 1953) that he did not necessarily advocate surrender to an aggressor. "The community of nations must reckon with unprincipled criminals who, in order to realize their ambitious plans, are not afraid to unleash total war. This is the reason why so many countries, if they wish to preserve their very existence and their most precious possessions, and unless they are prepared to accord free actions to international criminals, have no alternative but to get ready for the day when they must defend themselves. Even in these days, this right to self-defense cannot be denied to any state" (Cf. *Peace and War in the Judgment of the Church*, Karl Hormann, Newman Press, 1966: p. 60).

How does this square with Christ's suggestion that if a Christian is attacked, he should "turn the other cheek"? Jesus was talking about an individual Christian's reaction. The individual is certainly free to desist from defending himself or to try some form of passive resistance but a head of government seems to be in a different position. He cannot turn someone else's cheek. He has responsibility for the protection of his people and should not surrender that responsibility.

It seems clear that a war of aggression cannot be justified under any circumstances while a war of defense against unjust aggression may be justified. During the Vietnam war, debates on college campuses often revolved around the issue: is the United States an aggressor or a defender of a nation unjustly attacked? Opponents of our involvement attempted to show that the fracas in Vietnam was at the outset a civil war between revolutionary peasants in South Vietnam and the Saigon government, not a case of a foreign army invading from the North. For there was only one country, Vietnam. At the end of the Vietnamese war with the French, a military line had been drawn between the North and the South pending the outcome of a national election (which Diem refused to permit). There was no political line of division between the North and the South.

The U.S. contended that forces from the North had infiltrated into the South but it seems that the American intervention in South Vietnam had actually preceded any infiltration from the North. Senator Mansfield, for instance, said that even as late as 1965 when the U.S. escalated the war, there were only 400 Vietnamese from the North among the 140,000 enemy troops in South Vietnam. U.S. officials however contended that Communists from the North had instigated the original peasant uprising in the South and had continued to support the uprising in many ways.

This indicates how difficult it may be to prove that a war is a defense against unjust aggression, not a civil war. Of one thing we can be quite sure: if the conflict was originally a civil war between the peasants and Premier Diem, we had no right to intervene. On the other hand, if there was an actual invasion from the North aided and abetted by China and Russia, it might have been considered a foreign invasion of Vietnam, committed by Russia, China and Vietcong "stooges." In that case, our entrance into the war was a case of helping the South Vietnamese to defend themselves against unjust aggression. At any rate, it was up to the American citizen to read abundantly on the whole history of the affair in order to make a good judgment. He had plenty of eye-witness reporting of the war on TV and in the press, and he had numerous books by competent Far East experts which he could read in order to inform his conscience. The problem of sifting fact from rumor, slant from insight, was enormously complex. What increased the difficulty was that a credibility gap developed between the American people and the Government and many Americans found it hard to believe official accounts of what was going on in Vietnam. All this, however, did not relieve Americans of the duty of making an effort to discover the truth. The war was a colossal tragedy for all concerned and it demanded a colossal amount of study and meditation.

It is sometimes said that no defensive war can be tolerated today because every war might develop into a nuclear war. As we will see later, no nuclear war can be justified. If a war would probably become a nuclear war, then it should be avoided by every possible means. But it is wrong to say that every war today will ultimately develop into a war fought with nuclear bombs. The war in Vietnam, the 1967 Middle East war, the 1971 India-Pakistan war did not become nuclear conflicts.

The third requisite for a just war is that the ruler must have a right intention. A ruler might conceivably have a good cause but might have in the back of his mind some very dishonorable intentions or motives. I would think that any national leader who launches a war without referring his grievances to the U.N. is by that very fact suspect of having wrong intentions. The U.S. did not refer the Vietnam problem to the

U.N. and was properly criticized for not doing so. Possibly it felt that such referral would be futile as Soviet Russia would use its veto or possibly the State Department thought the U.N. was simply not equipped to deal with a guerrilla war. Whatever the reason, the U.S. did not present the appearance of a nation exerting every effort to avoid a war in Vietnam.

Revenge is a bad intention. During World War II we often read bumper stickers carrying the words, "Remember Pearl Harbor!" Nations have been known to wage a war simply to humiliate a rival country: this too would be a bad intention. Powerful nations have at times started wars in order to put their military prowess on public display and to intimidate and warn other nations. The U.S., for instance, was suspected of intervening in Vietnam to exhibit its colossal air power in order to warn Red China to stay out of Vietnam. This was, of course, an unfair and incredible fable. No reasonable man would believe that the U.S. would stage an experiment in which hundreds of thousands of Vietnamese would die as guinea pigs. Nor is national prestige a valid motive for waging a war. The only right intention is a resolve to defend against an aggressor in order to restore peace.

The fourth condition is that the ruler must wage the war in accordance with natural and international law. *Natural law* forbids all those inhuman and barbaric acts which civilized people have condemned from time immemorial. Reasonable men and women in times past have conceded that military operations might accidentally cause the death of civilians as a side effect. But humanity has condemned and denounced as criminal the wanton and willful killing of civilians, the looting of their homes, the torturing and mutilation of war prisoners. *International law,* on the other hand, forbids numerous acts of war which nations have pledged by treaty not to commit. Some acts, such as the torture of prisoners, are forbidden by natural law and also by *international law* to nations that have signed the treaties.

One of the war crimes condemned most severely by natural law is the wanton killing of civilians. Vatican II, as already mentioned, said that the indiscriminate bombing of cities is a crime against God and man deserving of unhesitating condemnation. The Council had in mind, of course, the civilians that would be killed in an indiscriminate attack on a city. Osgood and Tucker, in their *Force, Order and Justice* (p. 210) note that many nations claiming to reject the theory of collective guilt actually practice it. The theory of collective guilt is that a whole nation may be judged guilty and punished for war crimes. When one nation indiscriminately bombs a city and kills civilians belonging to the other country, it is implicitly saying that these civilians should be killed because they are guilty. If the bombing raid brings death only to a few, probably the attacking nation will not even bother to apologize, but if thousands are killed, the offending nation will not openly claim that the civilians were war criminals but that "military necessity" made the slaughter inevitable.

"Military necessity" is a handy term often used by military men to justify the murder of the innocent or the commission of almost any kind of atrocity. To the non-military, "military necessity" sounds very impressive and professional like the shoptalk exchanged by astronauts and Ground Control at Houston when they are heard over TV. It seems to say that anyone familiar with war should realize war is a dirty business and sometimes demands butchery. Consider all the things that "military necessity" is said to require—for instance, long-range weapons. With long-range weapons you cannot see the persons you kill. You simply follow instructions and drop the shells or the missiles or the bombs near the assigned target. You might have sympathy for a person you see face to face but how can you have sympathy for the civilian you can't see? You just fire away because "military necessity" demands it. You just do your job, no questions asked. Later on, you may hear how many civilians you have killed but you won't be upset. They are only statistics. You don't see the dying victims twitching in agony or the broken, bleeding bodies of the dead. In a very true sense, "military necessity" dehumanizes a man. Sad to say, our own country's record in this matter has not been good. The U.S. adamantly refused to hold the entire German people responsible for the Nazi war crimes and yet the U.S. did not hesitate to kill thousands of German civilians by indiscriminately bombing their big cities. One of the main reasons advanced for the bombing of these cities was to lower civilian morale but the bombing produced negligible results in this area. One interesting facet of the war was that Hitler was generally believed to be a madman yet he showed greater restraint in bombing big cities than did the British.

Formerly, national leaders used to explain away their slaughter of innocent civilians by saying that the civilians were really part and parcel of the war effort. Today the military and top government officials usually do not bother to apologize, apparently feeling that what happens to civilians is not a major consideration. After all, they say, "military necessity" demands that the main sources of the enemy's strength be destroyed in order to win the war, come what may to the civilians in the vicinity. While denying the theory of collective guilt they practice it with a vengeance.

From time to time an official has tipped his hand, asserting for instance that the Germans or the Japanese or the North Vietnamese must be taught a "lesson." The word "lesson," of course, means punishment. President Truman ordered the atom bomb dropped on Hiroshima. On that fateful day of the greatest human slaughter in all history, the President asserted that he used the bomb "against those who had attacked us without warning at Pearl Harbor, against those who had starved and beaten American prisoners of war, against those who had abandoned all pretense of obeying international laws of warfare" (Osgood and Tucker, *Force, Order and Justice,* p. 210). This, of course, was a barefaced lie. The President was taking liberties with the truth for the overwhelming majority of the victims at Hiroshima were civilians—the sick, the aged, women and children. To claim that they had attacked the American fleet at Pearl Harbor or that they had beaten and starved American prisoners was absolute nonsense. Later, in his *Years of Decision,* President Truman was more circumspect in his language. He said that he had intended that the bomb be dropped on a military target "to avoid, insofar as possible, the killing of civilians" (p. 420).

The crime of killing non-combatants assumes its most shocking form in the nuclear bomb. Walter Lippmann wrote in 1962: "Only a moral idiot with a suicidal mania would press the button for a nuclear war. Yet we have learned that, while a nuclear war would be lunacy, it is an ever-present possibility ("The Nuclear Age," *Atlantic Monthly,* May, 1962, p. 46). It is still a possibility and more fearful than ever since the number of nuclear bombs has increased so phenomenally. We have more than a thousand Minuteman intercontinental ballistic missiles, for instance. Some of these carry three nuclear bombs, each bomb being the equivalent of 250,000 tons of TNT.

President Johnson once said that in a few moments we can wipe out fifty to one hundred million of our enemies with our nuclear bombs and the enemy can do the same to us. Which means of course that in a nuclear war, we would be killing millions of Russian civilians. America itself would be almost totally destroyed, for Russia would retaliate and the resulting inferno would send our big cities up in flames. A nuclear war would not only be a crime against God and man for what it would do to one nation. The retaliation would mean that the two nations would be committing mutual suicide. A national leader who would press the button would be burying his own people.

It seems to be quite generally agreed that no nation has any right to start a nuclear war. As Lippmann said in 1962, "only a moral idiot with a suicidal mania would press the button." But what about our present American "deterrence policy"? We hold our nuclear bombs over the heads of the Russians as a threat to deter them from starting a nuclear war. We inform them in no uncertain terms that we possess an immense stockpile of nuclear bombs and that "we will let them have it" if they dare to drop a bomb on the United States. Defense Secretary McNamara told Congress in 1968 that we aim to deter other nations from attacking us by maintaining "our ability to destroy the attacker as a viable twentieth-century nation." Moreover, according to McNamara, we show our "unwavering will" to actually use our bombs.

Strangely, few Americans seem to register any protest against our deterrence policy. Possibly the war in Vietnam has distracted our attention from the threat to Russia. We were worried some years back, so much so that many Americans became almost hysterical to the point of buying bomb shelters for the back yard. Probably most Americans now feel that the deterrence policy is not such a bad idea. It has kept Russia from attacking us, hasn't it? Or perhaps some shrug off the whole question of the morality of the policy, claiming that the ordinary citizen is not responsible for national policy.

Let's take a look at the policy. Our Government is warning Russia and other nations that any nation dropping the bomb on us will be reduced to dust and ashes. Which means that America proclaims that we are ready to kill innocent civilians. That is a frightful promise coming from a nation that sometimes calls itself a Christian nation. But suppose we continue to make this promise but have no real intention of going through with such a threat? That is, suppose we are only bluffing. Bluffing is lying but I suppose many Americans would not lose much sleep over a lie. They would reason that bluffing does no harm in itself but might do a lot of good by preventing a nuclear war.

Bluffing, however, is risky business. Someone, some moral idiot, might press the button. America and Russia are terrorizing each other and terror, no matter how lightly felt, does fog the mind. I must confess I have no definite answer to this baffling question, however. The one impressive fact is that we have not had the war with Russia that seemed so imminent in the 1950s. Mutual terror seems to have preserved the peace. Winston Churchill once expressed it very aptly when he said, ". . . it may well be that we shall, by a process of sublime irony, have reached a stage in this story where safety will be the sturdy child of terror and survival the twin brother of annihilation."

To sum up, it seems clear that a nuclear war would certainly be a catastrophically immoral war. The deterrence policy, however, presents a dilemma. We tend to feel that the good end, peace, does not justify a bad means, lying. Yet we are tempted to follow the advice of the wag who said, "At times we must rise above our principles."

As already stated, nations are bound not only by natural law but also by international law. The latter is contained in international treaties by which nations pledge themselves to refrain from certain war crimes. The killing of non-combatants is forbidden to all nations by natural law but is also forbidden by international law to those nations that signed certain treaties. The U.S. has signed various treaties relating to the humane conduct of war, notably the treaties called the Hague Convention of 1907 and the Geneva Conventions of 1929 and 1949. These treaties bind the U.S. to refrain from numerous war crimes, and they bind with the highest authority because our international treaties become "the supreme law of the land." In pledging itself to honor these treaties, the American Government was not binding itself to some visionary or romantic line of conduct but merely to rules that represent a bare minimum of civilized behavior in war. They are rules which statesmen have gathered over the centuries as a result of moral shock at the atrocities committed by fighting men.

Some of the war crimes which the signers of these treaties have promised to avoid are the murder of prisoners, cruel treatment of the wounded, the use of torture to obtain information, the taking of hostages. The cruel treatment of prisoners would include suffocation, drowning and disfigurement as well as brutal methods of interrogating them.

These treaties bind the U.S. to refrain from inflicting any undue hardships on civilians such as burning down their crops, spraying their fields with chemicals that kill crops for years to come, forcing civilians to become refugees in overcrowded and unsanitary camps, arresting them en masse in order to terrorize them into making confessions, destroying their hospitals, punishing entire villages suspected of collaborating with the enemy. Many of these laws of war were invoked by the Nuremberg Court in the trials of Nazi war criminals after World War II. In 1946 the General Assembly of the U.N. unanimously approved the principles recognized by this Court. The U.S., therefore, is bound to obey these laws not only because it signed the original treaties but also because it joined in the U.N. resolution approving the principles endorsed by the Nuremberg Court.

The judges at Nuremberg made it crystal clear that no member of the armed forces of any nation can commit a war crime and justify it on the ground that he was simply obeying the command of his superior officer. He is bound to disobey an unlawful order. The U.S. Army Field Manual which contains the laws of war binding American servicemen says explicitly that a soldier is bound to obey only lawful orders. (I once heard on TV a reporter interviewing pilots of B-52s, asking them if they were ever prompted to look into the lawfulness of a particular order to bomb a certain area where there might be civilians. I was shocked to hear one of the pilots say that he was there to do his job, not ask questions.) No American serviceman, therefore, can commit an atrocity or war crime and then plead that he had been ordered to do it. This principle seems altogether reasonable to us in peace time. Yet when war breaks out and passions are aroused, a soldier may feel that he is excused from obeying the letter of the law in the heat of battle. Indeed, citizens at home sometimes tend to minimize such atrocities, especially if the victimized enemy had a color of skin other than white. The usual comment is that the offending soldier can be excused because he was trying to do his duty or because the civilians may have been aiding the enemy.

The nation-wide protest against the conviction of Lieutenant Calley had a somewhat different motivation. Calley was court-martialed, and convicted on March 29, 1971 of the premeditated murder of at least 22 Vietnamese civilians in the village of MyLai. About 100,000 telegrams, running 100 to 1 against the verdict, arrived at the White House. Whereupon President Nixon intervened to block his imprisonment. The public, however, was not giving its stamp of approval to the atrocity. A Gallup poll showed that Americans disapproved the verdict by 8 to 1 but 70% said they objected because they felt that Calley had been made a scapegoat for higher military and government officials who were more guilty than Calley.

This brings up the question of the guilt of higher

officials in war crimes. During the Vietnam war, peace leaders often condemned the policy makers in our federal government for directing the use of certain weapons. Article 22 of the 1907 Hague Convention forbids belligerents in war "to employ arms, projectiles or material calculated to cause unnecessary suffering." According to these peace people, a number of anti-personnel weapons used by the U.S. in Vietnam were forbidden by this treaty. Anti-personnel weapons are those designed not to destroy trucks or tanks but to injure or kill persons. Included among anti-personnel weapons are fragmentation bombs, projectiles, etc. that explode and spray out hundreds of thousands of steel, plastic or phosphorous-coated pellets or darts that lodge in the flesh. Usually the victims in Vietnam were persons in open, unprotected spaces. Frank Harvey in his *Air War—Vietnam* said that they were "the deadliest weapons used against the people in Vietnam." The *Gravel Mine* for instance sprayed out plastic pellets which could not be detected by x-ray and thus those wounded by this device found their injuries were harder to treat than wounds caused by steel pellets. According to the Nuremberg Court, not only government officials could be prosecuted for framing policies violating the Hague Convention but officials of corporations manufacturing the banned weapons could also be indicted.

The legality of these anti-personnel weapons used in Vietnam is a question that cannot be answered immediately. A thorough investigation, possibly a war crimes trial, will be necessary. During the war, all that anti-war activists could do was to call the attention of the public to these weapons and to register complaints to officers and stockholders of the companies manufacturing the weapons. The ordinary citizen, therefore, could make only a tentative judgment on the basis of reports and articles written by responsible and trustworthy experts.

To return to the Calley case, we may ask the question: what could possibly impel a young American to commit an atrocity such as that horrible butchery that took place at MyLai? One of the most plausible explanations is that offered by Dr. Robert Jay Lifton, professor of psychiatry at Yale University. Dr. Lifton says that the Vietnam war involved the young serviceman in a psychological state quite different from that experienced by soldiers in other wars. The typical young soldier went to Vietnam thinking he would have to confront a clearly-defined invading army as the war had been described to him as "an invasion from the North." Arriving on the scene, however, he found himself in a guerrilla war in which he could discover no well-defined military force, no group formations, no way to contact the enemy. Instead he found himself in a milling revolution, with the Vietcong, the North Vietnamese and the Saigon troops and peasants all looking very much alike. The enemy was invisible: it was everyone and no one. Seeing his buddies killed around him, he felt frustrated and frantic. His anger boiled. In his confused rage against all Vietnamese he began to suffer under the illusion that by gunning down someone—young or old, man, woman or child—he would finally succeed in making contact with the enemy.

This is only an educated guess, of course, but it seems quite plausible to me. Dr. Lifton is uniquely qualified to discuss the predicament of the war veteran because he has done psychiatric work at many veterans' hospitals (as well as research in Red Chinese brainwashing). We can have a measure of sympathy for men like Calley and yet we must not abandon the laws of war or war will become far more brutal than it is now.

The fifth requirement for a just war is: the ruler must have reasonable grounds for believing that the good to be achieved by the war will outweigh the evils that will result from it. This principle applies not only at the outset of the war but at every moment in its progress. As soon as a war becomes so destructive that it is obvious that the evil results will overbalance the benefits, at that moment the war certainly becomes unjust. Many Americans supported our involvement in the Vietnam war until they became convinced that the price in death and devastation on both sides was too high to justify our continuing the war.

The ordinary citizen cannot be expected to gather reams and reams of data and documentary evidence before making his decision as to the morality of a war. Knowing the history of wars in the past we can rightfully work on the presumption that a war is unjust unless the evidence in favor of its justice proves it just beyond a reasonable doubt. I agree with Roland Bainton who says in his *Christian Attitudes Toward War and Peace* that war "ought to be so overwhelmingly right as to manifest the will of God or else not right at all" (p. 242). A war cannot be right by a shade, say by 51% as against 49%. Only if there is an overwhelming preponderance of evidence in its favor can we participate in a war. To be just under the Just War theory, the war must fulfill all six conditions, but it seems to me that it would not be enough to find the war fulfilling each condition by a hair's breadth. The whole weight of cumulative evidence must prove the war moral beyond the shadow of a doubt.

In comparing the contemplated evils with the hoped-for benefits of the war we seek first to discover what the war will do or is doing to our own country, to our allies, to our troops. Will it demand the expenditure of vast sums of money that could be better spent on our country's poor, on purification of the country's rivers, streams and sources of water, on cleaning up the landscape, on educating the needy, on combatting crime so that citizens may walk the streets at night without fear? Many political experts felt that India was justified in invading Pakistan on December 3, 1971 not only because the invasion helped the East Pakistanis but also because it relieved India of the burden of supporting millions of Pakistani refugees who had swarmed into India after the West Pakistanis attacked. In considering a war in which America will be involved, we can ask: will this war relieve us of burdens or will it add to our burdens and problems? We do know it has relieved us of $104 billion dollars.

What will it do to our troops? Probably our policy planners never suspected what the Vietnam war would cost in American casualties but they should have anticipated the cost. They were the planners. Our total casualties were about 350,000. We lost almost 50,000 dead. How many returned with an addiction to drugs? How many came back suffering all kinds of psychological illnesses and aberrations?

What will the war do to the Vietnamese who were allies? The planners should have anticipated the 480,-000 casualties among the South Vietnamese fighting men, the 350,000 civilians killed—of whom 30% were children under 13 years of age—not to mention the plight of the 6 million refugees in South Vietnam and the unknown totals in Laos and Cambodia.

In counting up the evils that may come from a war, we should also count the cost to the enemy. What would the war cost the North Vietnamese and the Vietcong? I'm sure the planners did not count this cost. We tend to forget the enemy's casualties when we start thinking about launching a war, especially if the enemy has a different skin color, but we cannot say that our lives are more precious than theirs, if we want to remain Christian. Human life, American or Vietnamese, is of inestimable value. Fortunately a new "theology of the enemy" is beginning to develop in America and may eventually reach the offices of the policy planners. It contends that a civilized nation must make every effort to protect enemy lives during a war, preserve the society of the enemy during hostilities and rebuild the enemy country after the war.

Unfortunately, we have very few statistics on what the war has done to North Vietnam and the Vietcong. We can be quite sure, however, that their losses in human life, in crop destruction, in physical and mental health were colossal. If our government figures are correct, especially in regard to the so-called "body count," it would seem that their casualties ran about ten to every one American-South Vietnamese casualty.

We have considered costs. Now let us consider the benefits we hoped to achieve by the war. As soon as the costs began to overbalance the benefits to be achieved in Vietnam, the war would become unjust. As I have already said, the American Bishops in November, 1971 agreed that regardless of other considerations, any further American involvement could not be justified. "At this point in history it seems clear to us that whatever good we hoped to achieve through continued involvement in this war is now outweighed by the destruction of human life and of moral values which it inflicts. It is our firm conviction, therefore, that the ending of this war is a moral imperative of the highest priority." Many Catholics wondered why it had taken the Bishops so long to come to a conclusion that had been evident years earlier to ordinary citizens who had no professional acquaintance with moral theology.

What did the leaders of our government envision as the benefit they hoped to gain for the South Vietnamese? Contrary to the general impression, their stated purpose was not to stop Communism. They declared that the Vietnamese were free to choose their form of government, pointing out that they could choose Communism if they cared to do so, as that was their business. But the U.S. said that our aim was to make sure that the Vietnamese had free elections and that we had gone to Vietnam to insure freedom from Communist coercion at the ballot box. Free elections are indeed a great and admirable benefit. As the war progressed, however, Americans began to wonder if all the death and devastation we were inflicting on Vietnam was worth the free elections. For the elections would present a choice of a Communist ticket or candidates from the Thieu regime in Saigon, an outrageously corrupt political body.

I realize that I have unduly simplified, due to space limitations, the whole principle of proportionality, the balancing of prospective benefit against anticipated costs. I suppose no principle is ever as simple in application as it seems on paper but the important task here is to make the principle clear.

The sixth and final condition is: the ruler must try by every possible means to arbitrate the quarrel before starting a war. If he fails to do so—time permitting—the war is unjust. Sometimes the leader of a nation needs a lot of courage to resort to arbitration when his people are clamoring for war. Some hardliners will accuse him of compromising or selling out to the enemy but the genuine statesman will ignore the warmongers. If arbitration fails, he should refer the quarrel to the U.N. in spite of the fact that the warmongers will denounce the U.N. as a debating society or a nest of spies. The U.N. cannot expect to be perfect, reflecting as it does the nations of the world with all their good and evil. It is, however, our best hope for the prevention of wars, and many budding quarrels have been settled in the delegates' lounge as well as in the assembly hall.

What is the status of the Just War theory among thoughtful men and women today? It seems to be more popular with a few Catholic thinkers than with Protestant or Jewish leaders or secular scholars. Ralph Potter, in his "Conscientious Objection to Particular Wars," *Religion and the Public Order,* Cornell Univ. Press, No. 4: 1968, scores those churchmen who avoided the rigorous intellectual task of reflecting on the circumstances in which a Christian may take part in violence for the sake of the common good. "The Just War doctrine was not simply spurned, it was attacked as a specious form of casuistry . . ." (p. 75). The result was that when America got into the Vietnam war, many clerics knew no way of judging the morality of a war. Potter goes on to say that those who had heaped disdain on the doctrine seemed startled when it was pointed out that the arguments they used to condemn

American involvement in Vietnam were restatements of the conditions of Just War theory.

One puzzling fact is that Vatican II did not make any reference to the Just War theory in its document dealing with war and peace. Was it because the Bishops realized that certain national leaders in the past had found it easy to deliberately misinterpret the conditions of the theory in order to justify their nation's wars? Or was it that some felt that the title (Just War theory) gave the false impression that most wars are just? But why abandon a theory that is essentially good and helpful simply because men have misused and exploited it? Millions of mistakes have been made in mathematics but that is hardly a good reason for abandoning the theory. The problem with the Just War theory is not the theory itself but the bias or dishonesty with which certain persons have applied the test for a just war.

Can we abandon the theory because war is becoming more and more unpopular? There is no doubt that war is becoming unpopular because of the increased destructiveness of modern weapons or because common sense tells us that war is a wasteful and inefficient way to solve our nation's quarrels with a neighbor nation. But war's unpopularity does not seem to be reducing the frequency of wars. In this century alone the world has seen many wars. Why is this? Certain experts have ventured the opinion that leaders often fool their people by giving them high-sounding excuses for making inexcusable war on a neighbor nation. They offer very grandiose justification for wars. So, when it comes to the question as to whether the resultant evils will outweigh the benefits, they simply exaggerate the good they hope to accomplish. In starting up a little brush-fire war they announce, for instance, that this is a war to save humanity or to defend religion and civilization or to fight for God against Satan.

When some leader starts a war against a Communist nation or a rebel faction, the emotional anti-Communist may view it as a struggle against the enemies of God and religion. The official American goal in Vietnam was to insure free elections for the Vietnamese but many anti-Communists played up our involvement as a holy war against godless Communism. They said that what appeared to some Americans as a civil war between two Vietnamese factions should be viewed as a holy war against international Communism. And what was international Communism? They claimed it was a vast global movement which aimed to engulf the whole world beginning with tiny Vietnam. Now, anyone who sincerely believes he is fighting a worldwide diabolic conspiracy will probably pay little attention to the question of weighing the benefits and the evils of war. He will probably say that there should be no calculating the price, no haggling over cost when one is fighting for God and the freedom of humanity. He will insist that we should be ready to give up everything in this struggle against the godless Communists, even our lives to the last man. The enemy of God and man must be destroyed no matter how many casualties!

The "holy war," therefore, is a dangerous and deceptive illusion. A person who believes he is fighting a "holy war" loses his common sense and his conscience goes out the window. Christians who went on the Crusades usually imagined that their motives were pious but in most cases less honorable motives eventually prevailed over the pious motives. Many Crusaders became almost subhumanly cruel in fighting the "infidels." In most wars, soldiers try to punish the enemy for what he has done but the Crusader tried to punish the enemy for what he was—an "enemy of God." He lapsed into savagery without any twinge of conscience because he imagined he was fighting for God and felt that nothing could be too good (or too bad) for God. When Jerusalem was conquered by the Crusaders, one holy man wrote: "Some of our men (and this was more merciful) cut off the heads of their enemies; others shot them with arrows, so that they fell from the towers; others tortured them longer by casting them into the flames. . . . in the temple and portico of Solomon, men rode in blood up to their knees and the bridle reins. Indeed, it was a just and splendid judgment of God that this place should be filled with the blood of the unbelievers when it had suffered so long from their blasphemies" (Raymond of Agiles, quoted by Roland Bainton in *Christian Attitudes Toward War and Peace,* Abingdon, p. 112).

There is an old and very true Latin maxim—"Corruptio optimi pessima"—"the corruption of the best is the worst." When religious men are corrupted to hate, this is the worst type of degradation. A Christian, therefore, should take a cool and skeptical view of any attempt to publicize a war as a war for God and humanity. It is usually an attempt to break down, under false pretenses, the soul's orientation to peace. Robert Osgood says: ". . . tender consciences find in broader, more exalted goals a kind of moral compensation for the enormity of war and a rational justification for their contamination with evil. Thus the very ideals that proscribe war become an incentive for fighting war. An aversion to violence is transmuted into the exaltation of violence" (*Limited War,* Robert E. Osgood, Univ. of Chicago Press, 1957, p. 33).

V
The Anti-War Movement

"Let peace reign in the world. Never again war, never again. No more rivalry, contention, oppression, and egoism—no more. In their stead let there reign universal brotherly love in justice and freedom." These words of Pope Paul to the United Nations express not only the declared goals of the peace movement but also the secret aspirations of all humanity.

The Need of Peacemakers

In many places, peace is a seed buried deep in the human consciousness but needing careful attention and cultivation if it is to become a giant tree spreading its branches over the human family. Young people especially feel this yearning for peace. Green is the color of hope and hope springs eternal in the youthful heart, the hope that the green spring will return after the dead winter, the hope that the devastated battlefields of the world will soon be overgrown by green grass and clover. Youth was the most enthusiastic element in the anti-war movement in the last ten years. When their elders were only too ready to resign themselves fatalistically to war it was the young people whose protests roused an apathetic public.

Some young people, however, are tempted to say to themselves: "This anti-war movement is a wonderful cause but my contribution would be so tiny that it would never be noticed." It may seem small in contrast to the immensity of the military establishments throughout the world but each individual's effort, in concert with the efforts of thousands of other individuals, can become a mighty counter-movement to the forces of death. After all, the warmakers are well-organized. Think of the thousands of men and women in factories whose individual efforts synchronize into the manufacture of B-52's, transcontinental missiles, nuclear bombs and Poseidon submarines. Is there any reason why peacemakers should be apathetic, incapable of patient patient and sustained effort?

Vatican II was particularly anxious that the work of peace be not entrusted entirely to national leaders. The latter may be well-disposed to peace but find their efforts in that direction ineffective because of lack of public response. Therefore, the Council asked peacemakers to cooperate with the leaders by helping to stir up public interest and improve public attitudes toward peace. It cited the work that can be done by educators in instructing people in "fresh sentiments of peace" but the Council also urged everyone to "have a change of heart" in regard to tasks that can be done in unison for the betterment of our race. It is painfully true that the general public usually prefers business as usual and prefers to sleep on disturbing issues. It needs prophets and gadflies, young and old, to waken the sleepers.

Why So Few Catholic Protesters?

Why is it that so few Catholics in the past refused

to take part in wars that were obviously, almost ostentatiously unjust? One reason was a wrong concept of conscience that was prevalent in the past. Gordon Zahn has told the story of Franz Jagerstatter, an Austrian Catholic, who was executed in 1943 for adamantly refusing to serve in Hitler's army because he believed that Hitler's war was unjust. Before making his decision, Jagerstatter had sought guidance from priests and even from his Bishop. After he was arrested by the Nazis, the clergy who had advised him not to refuse induction into the service visited him in prison and persisted in urging him to change his mind, saying he should revoke his decision on the ground that he had a responsibility to his family. They insisted, moreover, that he had no right to question the morality of his country's wars. I would like to think these clergy were in good faith but the Jagerstatter narrative does show the need of a careful investigation of national wars by the citizens of the nation.

How did these clergy ever arrive at such a position? They probably based the notion that a man should not question his country's wars on the old idea that a military officer enjoyed a "presumption of right" in his favor when laying down a military command. That is, a soldier had no right to question an officer's order because there was a presumption that the officer was right in giving the order. Hitler, the supreme military commander of the German army, was believed to have every right to issue commands to Germans. Therefore, the notion was that Germans must presume that Hitler was right in launching the war. We had exactly the same situation here in America when American citizens said that no one should question the various Presidents' right to prolong the Vietnam war. Vatican II, however, made short shrift of this "presumption of right." The Bishops felt that the principle had been grossly abused and should be rejected. They wanted to stress the inviolable character of a rightly-formed conscience as well as the fact that blind obedience is no excuse for carrying out an order that violates conscience.

Possibly the Vatican II Bishops took a cue from the Nuremberg Court which had refused to accept blind obedience as an excuse for having committed war crimes. The Nuremberg Court had ample precedent for its position. Centuries before, St. Thomas had spoken about "indiscreet obedience" that obeys all orders indiscriminately—whether good or bad. Pope Pius XII had said in 1953: "There is no right to order an immoral act; there exists no right for this at all, no obligation and no permission to perform an immoral act even if it is commanded, even if refusing to act brings the worst possible personal harm" (Address to the Sixth International Congress of Penal Law: October 3, 1953). Vatican II declared without any ifs, ands or buts: "Therefore, actions which deliberately conflict with these same (moral) principles, as well as orders commanding such actions, are criminal. Blind obedience cannot excuse those who yield to them" (*Constitution on the Church in the Modern World,* n. 79: "Curbing the Savagery of War"). The Council went on to say that the courage of those who fearlessly resist men who order the extermination of an entire people or ethnic minority "merits supreme commendation." One of the Council Bishops specifically praised Franz Jagerstatter for his refusal to participate in a war of extermination.

Who Should Protest?

Anyone who is convinced in conscience that a war is unjust must register his or her protest in some fashion. Some Americans have the notion that men facing induction must become conscientious objectors but that everyone else is free to keep his mouth shut and "stay out of trouble." The fact is that everyone convinced of the injustice of a war should register a protest—insofar as he or she can do so. For everyone, except non-combatants such as invalids, aged persons and infants, is usually involved in the war effort in wartime, however slight his contribution may be. Gordon Zahn contends that it was not only those who burned civilians in the concentration camps who were guilty of war crimes but also the businessmen who designed the Nazi ovens or contracted to deliver the poison gas, the doctors who selected the victims, the locomotive engineers who drove the trains to the crematoria and the soldiers who guarded the trains to prevent the escape of the intended victims. The aged and the sick and the infant cannot be expected to make an outcry about the injustice of the war but others should protest according to the degree in which they are involved in the war effort. He who knows a war to be unjust and willingly takes part in it is taking some part in the sin and crime of murder.

The ordinary citizen may allege that he went along hesitatingly with a war because he had only a limited access to the facts. But no person can ever expect to discover all the facts, especially if he is aware that there is a credibility gap between himself and his government. He can make an honest and conscientious decision as to the justice of a war if he has made a reasonable attempt to find out the facts.

The Need of Prophets

In most countries of the Western world, the great majority of the population has supported most of its nation's wars. This is especially true of democracies: the people elect their representatives and tend to trust them precisely because they have elected them. Under dictatorships ruled by fear, the people usually follow the leaders even though they don't trust them. In short, most people follow the crowd in supporting the government. When the majority opinion supports a war, the temptation of most citizens is to look down their noses at any upstart who steps out of line. They regard him as an eccentric, a "nut," a poseur or Commie or perhaps a headline hunter.

This rule by the majority is nothing new. It is a problem that existed in the time of the Old Testament. The majority in ancient Israel often took part in some popular vice or abuse, worshipping false gods or indulging in the sexual perversions in vogue at the time. At these moments, prophets often appeared on the scene to bring the people back to their senses and force them to realize that they had been misbehaving, and that the custom or craze they had adopted was "dirty business" in God's eyes. In short, the prophets reminded the Jewish people of their conscience. They reminded them that defrauding widows and withholding wages from workers might be common practice but bad business. Those prophets pulled no punches. They condemned and denounced and excoriated the culprits, whether farmers or fishermen or priests or kings. Sometimes they were stoned to death.

So, too, God is raising up prophets today. Sometimes they dress unconventionally or act unpredictably but then some of the Hebrew prophets did strange things. The hierarchy of Bishops exists to discern whether or not a certain person has a genuine gift of prophecy but the Bishops must not extinguish the Spirit in the prophet. For the Holy Spirit does give inspirations to prophets to judge and condemn evils in the Church.

Yet there are prophets that speak to the world as well as to the Church. No longer do we picture God sitting on a cloud far away in the heavens. Now, since Vatican II especially, we realize that God is very much alive and active in this world. He speaks through the great revolutions of our time, notably the civil rights revolution, and he speaks through prophets. A prophet proclaims justice and condemns injustice. Can we not describe as prophet the journalist who kept proclaiming that Americans had committed a terrible atrocity at MyLai until the American public finally believed him and demanded an investigation. Was he not a prophet who revealed our part in the Vietnam prison system called "the tiger cages"? Even though we might disapprove of some of their actions, can we not call Father Daniel and Father Philip Berrigan prophets? Prophets do annoy the ordinary citizen who wants everyone to act as the ordinary citizen acts and prophets do occasionally make mistakes. But the true prophet shouts from the housetops his protests against any injustice to any member of the human family.

A duly elected government deserves respect but it will lose respect if it ceases to be respectable. The modern prophet's task is to keep reminding all governments, as Christ reminded Pilate, that all power comes from God and that a government enjoys authority only if it conforms to the law that comes from above. On the doors of certain medieval cathedrals are figures of kings going down to hell for having violated the law of God. The ancient Jewish prophets did not restrict themselves to ecclesiastical affairs. They ranged far and wide, reaching to politics and public policy, to high priests and Roman officials and kings. I hope that God will raise up more and more prophets to denounce wars with all the courage and fervor of Isaiah and Jeremiah. If it means denouncing national leaders, so be it. For after all, the more authority a ruler possesses, the more responsible should he be to the laws of God and the needs of men.

I suppose that among the growing ranks of peacemakers, false prophets will arise from time to time. It will not always be easy to distinguish the true peace prophet from the false one. Each of us, however, must use his God-given intelligence to discover the true prophet. Therefore, we have to steer clear of the notion that a man is a false prophet simply because he differs from the majority. It is precisely because the majority is often wrong that God sends a prophet and endows him with a special charism. No need to fear that there will ever be an oversupply of prophets. It is a thankless job and one that will be evaded by the false prophet. The true prophet has a sensitive awareness of his personal responsibility: he fears to abuse the special gift God has given him and thus do immense harm to the people God wants him to serve.

The Voices of Dissent

I have devoted a considerable amount of text to the subject of prophets? Why? Because the true prophet can be of immense help to us in forming our consciences on the justice of a war. The natural tendency is to dismiss dissenters as troublemakers, screwballs, self-appointed guides with a special pipeline to God. But history tells us that today's dissenters are often tomorrow's saints and heroes. They deserve a hearing. We may find they have startling new insights and broad global perspectives on the whole subject of war and peace. We cannot properly form conscience unless we look for information in the most unexpected places as well as in the official source-books. There is that whimsical Irish expression, "Look for the lost article in the place you'd never expect to find it!" The contemporaries of Jesus never expected to find a prophet in Nazareth, and Jesus himself said that a prophet has no honor in his own country.

The Treacherous Trap

Peacemakers who dissent from our national policy of piling up arms as a means of insuring national security are often viewed with suspicion in many quarters. Vatican II, however, said that the arms race is "an utterly treacherous trap." It is a trap in that it tempts us into thinking that more and more arms will make America more and more secure against foreign invaders or enemy planes and missiles. The fact is that the arms race only heats up the climate of war, creating the mood for war and increasing the very evil the arms race is designed to prevent.

It may sound highly unrealistic to talk about ending the arms race. For years, international conferences have been held to try to control the production of weapons of war. One notable series of talks was the set of conferences that led 47 states in 1972 to sign a pact outlawing biological warfare. The U.S. and Soviet Russia were among the states that promised "not to develop, produce, stockpile or otherwise acquire or retain" biological agents or toxins except for peaceful purposes. These 47 states also promised to continue negotiations for a ban on chemical weapons. We can hope and pray that the 1972 ban on offensive and defensive military weapons will eventually prove fruitful but in the meantime peacemakers should continue to protest against the arms race. We can be sure that powerful lobbies in Washington, representing weapons manufacturers, will not relax their efforts to keep the arms race going. These lobbies constantly warn the legislators that terrible catastrophes will afflict America if we let down our defenses against foreign powers. So we keep piling up munitions year after year. At the present time we have enough nuclear weapons to kill every Russian three times and we have the dubious honor of leading the world in the sale of weapons to foreign nations. No wonder the Second Vatican Council called the arms race "an utterly treacherous trap."

The American deterrence policy is the natural consequence of the arms race. In the 1950s we decided that the best way to handle the Russians was to arm ourselves to the teeth, pile up more and more weapons, and then let them know that we would retaliate immediately with a shower of nuclear bombs if they dared to attack us. The deterrence policy has been described by some critics as "blackmail," a term not altogether inappropriate. Others have called it "a gangster tactic." This policy, however, presents a new moral problem to which theologians have as yet failed to offer any consensus for or against. It is a policy we accept hesitatingly and with regret.

Catholics and the Anti-War Movement

Among the various groups working for peace in recent years are certain organizations with a religious orientation. One of the oldest is *The Fellowship of Reconciliation*. It has long been successful in bringing Roman Catholics into cooperation with members of other churches in the cause of peace. *Seminarians for Peace* originated at Yale Divinity School as an anti-Vietnam war organization. *The Resistance* is a loosely-structured group that includes many seminarians. Probably the most active of the ecumenical peace groups is *Clergy and Laymen Concerned*. It is not committed to rigid strategies but encourages members to engage in anti-war activities that seem appropriate to their local situations. *The American Friends Service Committee* has action groups that stress non-violence. *The Center for Non-Violence* is an ecumenical group community for peace.

Among the activist Catholic groups, the best known peacemakers have been the dedicated men and women connected with *The Catholic Worker*. The publication became an outstanding voice for peace during the Spanish Civil War (1936-39) when it opposed General Franco's "holy crusade." This roused the ire of many Catholics but Dorothy Day continued her editorial work appealing to Catholics to practice and encourage non-violence. Out of *The Catholic Worker* came the American Pax Association and the Catholic Peace Fellowship. *The Catholic Worker* had a strong influence on Fathers Daniel and Philip Berrigan: through the magazine they became affiliated with the Catholic Peace Fellowship. Pax publishes *Peace* quarterly.

The religiously-oriented peacemakers have focused a strong light on the frightful destructiveness war brings to human life and the material fabric of the planet on which we live. Their attitude can be summed up in the words of a pioneer peacemaker: "Our existence on this wonderful planet is too short and too beautiful for us to give any earthly power that right which, from the beginning, has belonged only to the unsearchable. The sacredness of human life—alas not as reality and fact—but still as idea and what we look forward to—is the basis of our critical and political thoughts and therefore our pacifism" (Quoted by F. Stratmann in *Church and War,* 1928, p. 153).

While individual Catholics, especially young priests and nuns, played a large and much-publicized role in the radical peace movement during the Vietnam war, the surprising fact is that Catholics have made a very small contribution to the general peace movement in proportion to their numbers. It is surprising because many of the recent popes have been ardent advocates of the cause of peace and American Catholics have traditionally been attentive listeners to papal statements. I realize that they don't give papal pronouncements the instant assent they offered previously and yet it is puzzling why American Catholics generally seem to be indifferent to papal views on peace.

Pope Benedict XV, for instance, worked incessantly for peace during World War I but European Catholics paid scant attention and American Catholics were also rather cool to his pleas. Pope Pius XII followed in the footsteps of Benedict. (In fact, in the summer of 1917 as a papal representative he had gone to the field-headquarters of the Kaiser on the western front, presenting him with a letter from Pope Benedict urging the Kaiser to restore peace.) Although he wrote reams of letters on peace while he was Pope, he seems to have been a voice crying in the wilderness as far as American Catholics were concerned. Pope John is known of course for his influential encyclical entitled "Peace on Earth" but it was apparently taken more seriously by many non-Catholics than by Catholics. Pope Paul has also worked hard for peace and his address to the U.N. pleading for peace was one of the high moments of the twentieth century. Yet the Vietnam war was in progress at the time and American Catholics seemed to think he was not talking to them but to the Vietnamese Communists. They apparently took it for granted that America was fighting a just war. His talk to the U.N. did not make a dent in American Catholic opinion on the war, except in the case of a few young Catholics here and there.

Various small Catholic groups, consisting of priests or nuns or laity, attracted a great amount of public attention during the Vietnam war by staging dramatic anti-war protests. Some demonstrated at draft board offices, some at induction centers or in Catholic churches during the liturgy. They bore witness to the Gospel of peace in this spectacular fashion because they felt they had to shock clergy and parishioners out of their apathy to the bloodshed in Vietnam. It is often said that these provocative episodes, especially those in which government property was destroyed or the liturgy interrupted, did more harm than good to the peace movement. Unquestionably, many middle-class Catholics were "turned off" by these protests, and this was probably a partial explanation of the general Catholic resistance to the anti-war movement. In fairness to the demonstrators, however, I think it must be said that they were more concerned about disturbing the consciences of the comfortable than about "winning votes." One persistent criticism was that such demonstrators were ready and willing to denounce American atrocities in the war but never the atrocities committed by the Vietcong—as if to say, why blame the American soldiers if the Vietcong were as bad or worse? Such criticism seems unrealistic. Has any warring nation ever listened to criticism from people on the other side? These demonstrators in Chicago or Baltimore or Milwaukee hoped to stir the consciences of local citizens: they were under no delusion that a protest in their neighborhood would be heard round the world in Hanoi.

Some Objections to Catholic Peacemakers

When discussing war and peace with our fellow Catholics in America, we can be quite sure that we will encounter certain common objections to Catholic participation in the peace movement:

1. Some say that peace is a political question and that a Catholic had better not mix religion with politics. Usually this objection comes from a person who feels that religion is almost exclusively a matter of personal salvation. Before Vatican II certain Bishops had as their motto, "Salus animarum suprema lex"—"the salvation of souls is the supreme law." *Personal* salvation is surely a major concern for all Christians but it must not be confused with *private* salvation. Our salvation depends largely on what we do for others. Scripture tells us that God will judge us at the last day on what we have done for the starving, the prisoners, the sick." "I tell you solemnly, insofar as you neglected to do this to one of the least of these, you neglected to do it to me" (Matthew 25, 45). Vatican II has brought us back to the original Christian perspective on salvation, that we please God and become perfect by doing things for others rather than by exclusive care and concern about our own spiritual life. Or rather, that true spirituality is life *for others*. Vatican II made clear, moreover, that Christians should not speak of saving souls but of saving persons who are a composite of body and soul. Religion pertains to persons, body and soul, and the ugly feature of war is that it ravages both body and soul. Religion does not relate to party politics or the machinery of political organization but it does relate profoundly to all injustices done to the neighbor, especially God's poor. If politics is responsible for war and war is responsible for the killing of poor peasants and the devastation of their land, then we must mix in politics. "We must obey God rather than men" as St. Peter said.

2. Another common objection, in this instance to lay participation in the peace movement, is that the laity should leave the final decision on all moral questions to the Church authorities. Bishops and priests, however, have enough to do without taking on the job of making moral decisions for the people. In confession, the penitent decides whether or not he committed a particular sin: the priest can advise him one way or the other but only the penitent can make the decision. Each individual must make up his own mind as to what he considers to be a personal sin. In judging a war, a Christian seeks the advice of priests perhaps, but he must also get advice from reading books by political experts, constitutional lawyers and from anyone else who has information that might help him make a decision about the morality of the war. Even the clergy, in making up their minds about the justice of the war, must consult laity who are skilled and versed in secular sciences. How can anyone make a moral decision on the Vietnam war without knowing the basic grievances of the peasants who rebelled against Diem, the legal status of the Tonkin Gulf resolution, the legality of our intervention in the war? In short, he must not shift the responsibility for making the decision to any Church officials, nor should he rely on Church officials exclusively for advice on the rightness or wrongness of the war.

3. There are Catholics who say that no one should aid and abet a selective conscientious objector, that is, one who objects not to all wars but to a particular war. Their reasoning seems to be: if you condemn all wars, that's a moral decision but if you condemn only a particular war, that's politics. In other words, approve or reject all wars but don't pick and choose. One legal expert has aptly described this argument as a matter

of discriminating against the discriminating. I realize that the Supreme Court has refused to exempt *selective* conscientious objectors but this smacks to me of Puritanism. The Puritan usually condemned all dancing, all card playing, all recreation on Sunday. The Catholic approach to moral questions is more discriminating: it says that some dancing is good, some bad: some card games are good, some bad. The goodness or evil of an act varies with the circumstances surrounding the act.

4. There are Catholics who say that conscientious objectors are necessarily rebels who disturb the peace and harmony of society. They label them "cowards" or "pinkos" or "nuts" and I feel sure they would go into convulsions if they happened to read President John F. Kennedy's remark: "War will exist until the distant day when the conscientious objector enjoys the same reputation and prestige the warrior does today." I have known devout Catholics who felt that the good Christian saves his soul by staying out of mortal sin, receiving the sacraments, doing what he is told and not "rocking the boat." Such a person does not object so much to conscientious objection as to disturbing the peace. Vatican II, however, did not exalt passive obedience over personal responsibility, personal initiative and social reform. The Council asked Christians to comfort the disturbed but also to disturb the comfortable, to band together with other Christians to protest against all injustices that hurt the poor and oppressed. It is necessary, therefore, to educate Catholics to the teaching of Vatican II on the need and obligation of resisting injustice. After pointing out precisely how Christians can change the world about them, the *Constitution of the Church in the Modern World*

says: "Therefore holding faithfully to the Gospels and benefitting from its resources, and united with every man who loves and practices justice, Christians have shouldered a gigantic task demanding fulfillment in this world. Concerning this task, they must give a reckoning to Him who will judge every man on the last day" (No. 93).

Is War Inevitable?

It is often said that war is inevitable because of human depravity. Most animals are thought to be driven by instinct to tear and claw other members of their species but man is said to take a deliberate delight in fighting wars and committing atrocities. War is not so much in his blood as in his free will; he fights wars because he likes wars, the more brutal the better. According to this notion, wars are inevitable because man in his savagery will murder and plunder his own kind as long as he is man, that is, until he becomes a new species that will love its own kind—a phenomenon that these fatalists say will never occur.

The ancient Greeks at times imagined that wars were inevitable because the gods drove men to war. Croesus once started a war which Herodotus was anxious to excuse because he saw the stupidity of it. So Herodotus blamed it on the gods. "No one is so foolish as to prefer war to peace in which instead of sons burying their fathers, fathers bury their sons, but the gods willed it so." The Greeks at times attributed all kinds of shenanigans to the gods.

Christians are not accustomed to blame wars on God (even though they do start holy wars for God).

Yet we do find many Christian fatalists who claim that wars are inevitable. Sometimes they will try to bolster the claim with the Scripture text in which Christ predicted that there will be "wars and rumors of wars." Actually he said that you will "hear of" wars and rumors of wars, not that there will be wars forever. This misuse of a Scripture text reminds me of Shakespeare's comment in *The Merchant of Venice*, III,2,78: "In religion, what damned error but some sober brow will bless it and approve it with a text."

Now, is it true that the innate violence in human nature drives men to fight in wars? Is it true that war is a manifestation of a biological instinct that men cannot control? I don't deny that most people have a violent streak in them. One of the characters in an Irish play says that "it's better to be fightin' than to be lonely." Even the most respectable among us enjoy Westerns and the movie, "The Godfather," the quintessence of violence. But I feel that we could study human psychological reactions for centuries before coming to a definite conclusion as to whether violence is inborn or acquired. The important question, however, is not whether man is violent but whether he can control his violence. Sure, violence will impel him to use force but the question is: will he keep on striving to attain some goal that can be attained only by an immoral resort to violence?

For all the evidence there is of a violent streak in human nature, I don't believe that man is by nature a killer. He can, however, acquire the taste for killing and it is unfortunately true that military training in wartime does teach and train men to kill. It is unfortunate that the armed services do train men to be good killers, that is, to teach them to overcome their inhibitions and put men to death. To become a killer, one must be carefully taught.

Moreover, there do seem to be certain conditions under which a man becomes less reluctant to kill. If the enemy is of a different race or color, men can persuade themselves that they are not really killing a human being but something that is subhuman. This was true in the Vietnam war when men killed peasants because they were "gooks" or "dinks" or "slant-eyed people." Even if the enemy is not of a different race or color, propaganda can make him out to be a monster. This was done in World War I but happily, propaganda was not quite as inflammatory during the Vietnam war.

In short, I do not think that there is a blood lust in all of us that makes war inevitable. No such deep-seated tendency toward violence has been proved by any respectable body of evidence. If the proficiency in killing that was exhibited by Americans in World War II or Vietnam was due to a wild streak in the blood, why did not returning veterans display this tendency after they returned home? I can remember the dire predictions during World War II in regard to American commandos who had been taught to strangle their enemies instantaneously and noiselessly. Calamity howlers contended that they would surely become cutthroats in peacetime. They did not. Why? Because killing was not to their taste. The messy business had been taught them but their better nature shook off all this grisly information. One can forget what he has been taught.

I once heard a noted American leader say that killing in war is something that comes from the dark side of the psyche, and he recommended that our government should enlist psychologists, sociologists and other scientists to find out how the sickness can be cured. I would think the money could be better spent in trying to persuade our national leaders to become more adroit at problem-solving. For most wars derive from stupidity and bad judgment rather than from passion. The worst blunders are often made by men with experience, expertise and humaneness who are just too proud to admit their blunders. What they lack is the humility to reveal they are not infallible and that expertise relevant to earlier crises may prove altogether useless in a new situation.

Wars are not inevitable because of a blood lust built into man's biology. Violence is not an incurable human disease: it is a tendency that can be controlled. With intelligence, compassion and the grace of God, war can be eliminated to a large degree. Men can be educated to peace. They can be shown how idiotic were most wars in the past. And they can be taught to love peace as the climate in which the children of the future will grow in wisdom and serenity. The child grows tall in the joy and quiet of nature, in the beauty of valleys and streams untouched by bombs, in the loveliness of sunset by a waterfall where never is heard the scream of rockets, the dreaded whirring of B-52s or the cries of refugees fleeing in panic before the advance-guard of the enemy.

VI
Obstacles to Sound Judgment

We have been dealing with general principles for the promotion of peace. We have to keep in mind, however, that promoting peace is no easy task. There are forces working against peacemakers, not so much the enemies of the peace movement but the hidden forces in the mysterious depths of the human mind. I have in mind the pet illusions that often prevent even the sincerest persons from grasping the horror and the immorality of most wars.

It is wrong to deceive another person but it is worse to deceive one's self and yet that is what is happening to many Americans. They have wrapped themselves in illusions about war and they hold on to these illusions as their security blanket. They give the impression of despising any anti-war workers but in many cases their cocksureness is only a front. Inwardly they are insecure and skeptical about their position on war but they hate to admit it outwardly as they feel that peacemakers and pacifists challenge the old patriotism they cherish. But the test of psychological maturity is the ability to study a new idea even though it runs counter to a popular notion. This mysterious mind of ours tries desperately to resist what is new and different but we cannot be honest with ourselves or with God unless we seriously investigate what we suspect may be the right way of thinking about war and peace. Our own personal experiences with our own hidden fears and feelings should remind us that there are similar factors that are hard at work in the subconscious of persons we are trying to win over to the cause of peace.

Neurotic Anti-Communism

One such mental block is the neurotic anti-Communism that can still be found in certain places in the U.S. There is a reasonable anti-Communism but I refer to that excessive fear of Soviet Russia that is utterly unreasonable. Fortunately it is relatively rare today, existing usually only in senior citizens who remember with fear and trembling the era of the 1950s when Soviet Russia was a gigantic threat to the peace of the world. Communion breakfast orators waxed a bit too dramatic over the threat but Soviet Russia was unquestionably a menace of monstrous proportions. In the 1950s Communism was a highly-disciplined, tightly unified, global movement commanding a seemingly irresistible military machine that had crushed the Nazi juggernaut and captured one country after another in Eastern Europe. When Josef Stalin snapped the whip at Moscow, every Communist leader throughout the world stood at attention.

Today Soviet Communism is still a mighty force, and a military power second only to the U.S. It is, however, nothing like the threat to world peace it was in the 1950s. Its compact unity has been fragmented. China, Yugoslavia and other Communist countries have asserted their independence of Moscow in varying degrees. The men in the Kremlin can press the button that can kill on first strike one hundred million Americans but there is a new friendliness between Russia and the U.S. Instead of reading Khrushchev's boast to John F. Kennedy that he would bury us, we now read that President Nixon toasted Russia at a state dinner and signed an arms limitation pact with the Russian leaders.

Young Americans, as I have mentioned already, tend to dismiss the threat of Soviet Communism as a figment of their elders' imagination but we do find a certain residue of this excessive anti-Communism even among young people in sections of America. Possibly the distrust and suspicion of Russia entertained by their parents brushes off on the young people. There is enough anti-Communism in some young minds to prevent them from taking a calm, cool look at Soviet Russia, but it is not the nervous, jumpy kind of anti-Communism that is found among some older citizens. There are no Archie Bunkers under 21 who see a Communist conspiracy behind long hair, lettuce boycotts and peace demonstrations.

It is imperative, for the sake of peace, that we gather as much accurate information as possible about Soviet Russia. To know is to understand. What are the Soviets trying to accomplish? What is their philosophy? How has Soviet Communism changed since the time of Lenin, and in what way has it remained the same? Because of the former prevalence of excessive anti-Communism, we seem to have erected a great mental wall of separation around everything in the Kremlin, and I have no doubt that some older Americans consider it treason to talk of developing a sympathetic understanding of Russia.

But if we continue to distrust and suspect the Soviets, if we get the jitters and become panicky every time they "rattle the sword," if we begin to feel that war with Russia is inevitable, we are most certainly sowing the seeds of war in our own hearts. There are good grounds for believing that America and Russia can "peacefully coexist." The term "coexistence" means that we will both renounce war as a way of settling our disputes, that we will not invade each other's territory, and that we will not interfere in the internal affairs of other countries. Positively, we will try to cooperate with Soviet Russia in trade, in cultural exchanges and scientific projects. Dare we trust Russia? Pope John, with his characteristic genius for piercing to the heart of an issue, wrote in his encyclical *Pacem in Terris:* "All must realize that there is no hope of putting an end to the building of armaments, nor of reducing the present stocks, nor still less—of abolishing them altogether, unless the process is complete and thorough and unless it proceeds from inner conviction: unless, that is, everyone sincerely cooperates to banish the fear and anxious expectation of war with which men are oppressed. If this is to come about, the fundamental principle on which our present peace depends must be replaced by another which declares that the true and solid peace of nations consists not in equality of arms but in mutual trust alone" (n. 113).

Those who like to consider themselves hard-headed realists would probably say that Pope John didn't have his feet on the earth when he wrote *Pacem in Terris*. But hard-headed realists were not very realistic when they got us involved in the Vietnam war. It was the paranoia of excessive fear of global Communism that landed us in the Asian morass. Some of the mutual trust recommended by Pope John could have kept us out of that imprudent military escapade.

Even now, as I already said, there are pockets of this anti-Communist paranoia in America. It is a phobia that will not disappear overnight. It is not realistic, however, to imagine we are surrounded on all sides by secret Communists, and that the only way to handle this threat is to get into a war and kill atheistic Communism. Vatican II urged us to "free ourselves from the age-old slavery of war." We might add a footnote to the effect that Divine Providence also urges us to shake off the last remnants of the paranoia of anti-Communism.

The Worship of Revolutionaries

A very different obstacle in the way of the peacemaker, the very reverse of anti-Communism, is the present idolatry of leftist revolutionary leaders of the Third World. (By Third World I mean the underdeveloped peoples of the world in contrast to the Free World and the Communist World.) Not only in Latin America but in the U.S. as well, university students and professional scholars have made heroes of men like Regis Debray, Che Guevara and Father Camilo Torres. This admiration for men of violence is a surprising development. Young intellectuals, revulsed by the Arab terrorists' slaughter of eleven Jewish athletes at the 1972 Olympics, deplored this ugly violence and bloodshed. Now, we find many sensitive young people as well as mature intellectuals expressing their ardent admiration for Marxist leaders who urge bloody revolution to liberate the poor in underdeveloped countries. This support of ruthless leaders can be heard even in ecumenical circles. Ecumenists at international meetings listen to confreres from Third World countries asserting their conscientious Christian resolve to participate in national and social revolutions involving the use of force and arms. After listening to these fighting words, most ecumenists realize that liberation is a very complex problem but hesitate to adopt a theology of revolutionary violence. The Conference on Church and Society (of the World Council of Churches) stated the problem confronting contemporary ecumenists: "Whether the violence which sheds blood in planned revolutions may not be a lesser evil than the violence which, though bloodless, condemns whole populations to perennial despair."

What should be our stand as peacemakers? Can we advocate violence in the U.S.? Having canonized non-violence, can we turn around and canonize violence? It seems to me that what is permissible for the Third World may not necessarily be permissible for the U.S. While our system of justice has its failings, it does generally listen to just grievances, and our government has been making some effort to help the poor. If the legal system completely deteriorated in the U.S., there could be a just cause for a violent revolution, but the situation has not yet become as intolerable as that. Violence can be used as a last resort for those denied justice but sympathy and solidarity with the poor would not ordinarily be sufficient reasons to justify a bloody revolution.

Here is a problem for the Christian. He must show

his sympathy for the poor and support their just demands but should the Christian disapprove of armed revolutions? The answer depends, it seems to me, on the particular circumstances surrounding the revolution. If, for instance, the probable evils resulting from an armed revolution outweigh the anticipated good results, then such a revolution cannot be approved. One Latin American observer said that 99% of bloody revolutions are unsuccessful. But if the tyranny of an unjust government is worse than a bloody revolution, and if a revolution seems likely to succeed in overthrowing the tyrannical regime, it might be approved.

The theology of revolution, however, has not yet been developed and it will probably be a few years before we have such a theology. In the meantime, the peacemaker would do well to scrutinize his or her admiration for a rebel leader. God is working underneath the great issues and revolutions of our time but sometimes it is hard to distinguish what God is doing from what is evil in the revolution. Like everything human, revolutions have their good features as well as their bad features and God is certainly not causing the evils. The rebel hero may actually be a demonic person even though he fights against a tyrannical government. That is why some revolutions bring about a worse situation than the original tyranny. Too often as the old maxim has it, "the persecuted becomes the persecutor." The rebel leader sometimes becomes the slave-driving dictator.

Father Camilo Torres, the guerrilla fighter for social justice in Colombia, is regarded as a great hero and revolutionary model by many young Christians. In 1967 he was ambushed as he tried to operate his machine gun near a little town in Colombia. As priest and social reformer, he had gradually become more and more convinced of the need of violence to bring about reform and as a result of his revolutionary activities he became an enemy of his government and was rejected by his ecclesiastical superiors. "The people know that only armed rebellion is left" said this young guerrilla-fighter. "The people are desperate and ready to stake their lives so that the next generation of Colombians may not be slaves." Father Torres insisted that Christians in Colombia had a stern obligation to join the revolution. "Every Catholic who is not a revolutionary and not on the side of the revolutionaries, lives in mortal sin."

Father Torres has been extravagantly praised as a martyr for his people but also condemned exuberantly as a rebel without a cause. What shall we say of him? I think we can admire his courage, his dedication, his capacity for sacrifice. I am not at all sure that we can praise his use of death-dealing weapons to achieve his goal of justice. Force might conceivably bring political freedom but it is no guarantee of economic freedom and his aim was to relieve poverty. Force does not bring food to the starving. Force does not bring to a hungry people the natural resources, the technology, the foreign aid that are necessary to feed them. A colorful figure Father Torres undoubtedly was, but I find it hard to picture Christ carrying a machine-gun. "Learn from me for I am meek and humble of heart." Archbishop Helder Camara, the great social reformer of Brazil, has been an ardent advocate of revolution but he has definitely ruled out violence as a means of transforming Brazilian society. It is not hard to picture this holy little man as the image of Jesus Christ.

Selective Inattention

A third obstacle in peacemaking is what is called "selective inattention." In trying to judge the rightness or wrongness of a war, conscience sometimes plays tricks on us. It may try to block out of our conscious vision certain facts or opinions that run contrary to a decision we would like to make. Psychiatrist Harry Stack Sullivan gave the term "selective inattention" to the psychological quirk by which the mind inhibits its curiosity about something. We give our undivided attention to facts that seem to bolster a judgment we want to make but we unconsciously exclude attention from those items that might make us change our minds.

Ralph K. White, a long-time student of the psychological causes of war who has made extensive studies in Communist public opinion, wrote an article entitled "Selective Inattention" for *Psychology Today* (November, 1971). He took six important questions bearing on the justice of our involvement in the Vietnam war, pointing out that a careful study of these questions would have dissuaded our policy planners from getting us into the war. Then he proceeded to prove from various documents and records that the designers of our national policy, except for Undersecretary of State George Ball, had never paid any attention to these questions. Their minds were made up and they did not want to read anything that might incline them to re-examine their decisions. They felt reasonably sure of their position so their minds unconsciously bypassed another line of thinking.

The first question, for instance, was: "When the United States was building up its involvement in Vietnam (between 1950 and 1967) was it going against what most politically conscious people in South Vietnam wanted"? The minds of men like John F. Kennedy, John Foster Dulles, Dean Rusk and others, did not look into this basic question. Why? Because they had already decided that the U.S. must "stop Communism in Asia." They had arrived at a reassuring degree of certainty they were right and some psychological mechanism closed their minds to what lawyers might call "newly discovered evidence."

I know many very sincere men who made up their minds about the morality of the Vietnam war in the early 1960s. Thereafter, they considered it a closed issue. They did not want to reopen the case perhaps because they felt they would be "vacillating" or "inconsistent" if they changed their opinion of the justice of the war. But a judgment on the morality of a national war is a terribly important matter not only for a young man who may have to become a conscientious objector but for every American who contributes by way of taxes or anything else to the war effort. The Holy Spirit gives us insights into important problems day after day. He does not hesitate to shed new light on these problems merely because we are already satisfied with our solutions. In the mass for Pentecost we pray to the Holy Spirit: "Bend the stubborn heart and will; melt the frozen, warm the chill, guide the steps that go astray." Only the arrogant man or woman would close his mind to an inspiration of the Spirit urging him to change his opinion on something. The Christian trying to make up his mind on the morality of a war re-examines his conscience day by day, aware that the Holy Spirit is constantly bringing to light new angles of the problem. Bull-headed stubbornness is just another form of pride and as St.

Thomas More used to say, "Pride is the mother of all mischief."

Superpatriotism

Finally there is "superpatriotism." This exaggeration of a natural virtue throws one's mental vision completely out of focus. It is natural to love one's country as it is to love one's family but patriotism can become inflated, especially these days when there is such a revival of excessive nationalism all over the world. The old maxim, "You can't have too much of a good thing," is absurd. Ask the victims of a flood. Patriotism is a great virtue as long as it is subordinated to God. If we attempt to put it first, we are making an idol of brass. "I am the Lord, thy God. Thou shalt not have strange gods before me."

Every government has the duty and right to protect its citizens in the secure enjoyment of their natural rights such as the rights to life, liberty and the pursuit of happiness. To protect its people from unjust aggression from an enemy, it has a right to use force under certain conditions. Vatican II recognized this right of self-defense. But the trouble is that many governments come to imagine they have an absolute, unconditional right to use force under any circumstances, claiming they have a sovereign right to do anything for the welfare of the nation.

This no Christian can accept. No nation is really sovereign if by "sovereign" you mean unlimited in power. Only God is sovereign: every nation and every person is subject to God's law. Any "superpatriot" who exalts the American government as a sacred thing worthy of worship is simply indulging in idol worship. Our weary world has suffered enough this century from dictatorships like that of Hitler, Mussolini and Stalin. Unfortunately our age has not yet learned to escape from "superpatriotism." As Robert Osgood and Robert W. Tucker say in their *Force, Order, and Justice:* "What seems characteristic of the present period is surely not a widespread and growing skepticism toward the state but the faith with which so many peoples have accepted the state, or the nation-state, as the principal institution for achieving a hoped-for destiny" (p. 324). God help us when our destiny is dictated by a tyrant!

The "superpatriot" cannot make an accurate judgment on the morality of a war because he has an exaggerated notion of the role of a government in the divine plan. On the other hand, the total pacifist seems to underrate the rights of government. He refuses to recognize that a government has any right to protect its people by force. To be realistic, the sad fact is that governments usually cannot protect their people except by the use of force to repel attacks. And a government that cannot defend its people is not really a government at all. Perhaps someone may say that no government today can successfully defend its people in a nuclear war. This is true but it is also true that the use of nuclear weapons to deter another nation from starting a war has been successful (at least until now) and this deterrence policy is an example of the use of force.

There are, however, few total pacifists. There is a superabundance of "superpatriots" in America, and their distorted view of the role of government spawns endless trouble in war time. The trouble is compounded when the government itself becomes "superpatriotic."

How can a government become "superpatriotic"? By overstepping its proper role as protector of its own people and aspiring to become the dominant power among the governments of the world. An American president a few years ago said: "We are the Number One nation and we are going to stay the Number One nation." In the context of his remark he was using government and nation interchangeably. Now if history tells us anything, it is that any nation that seeks not to serve but to dominate other nations eventually crumbles from within. National leaders would do well to take to heart Christ's advice to his apostles, "You know that the rulers of the Gentiles lord it over them and their great men exercise authority over them but with you it will not be so. On the contrary, whoever wishes to become great among you shall be your servant" (Matthew 20,25-26).

VII
The Draft

The draft is not a novelty in American history. The first draft laws were enacted during the Civil War when both the North and the South passed laws conscripting manpower. There are inequities in the present draft law but they are not as blatant as the injustices perpetrated by the North from 1863 on. Northern draftees could pay $300 to buy themselves the privilege of exemption from the draft. The poor, notably the Irish immigrants in New York City, reacted to this injustice by breaking out into a riot-protest in New York City in which the toll was reported to be 1,200 dead.

The first World War saw a return of the draft when the U.S. entered the war in 1917. It is an interesting fact that 300,000 "draft dodgers" were never tried for evading this law. Conscription returned once again in 1940 when Congress passed a draft act even before we got into the second World War. Except for a few very brief periods we have had a draft law ever since the second World War. The present Military Selective Service Act will remain in effect at least until June 30, 1973.

The Present Draft Act

The present Act is not very popular with Americans generally. During the Vietnam war there was never any danger to the U.S. itself and yet thousands were drafted into what many of them called "involuntary servitude." When the Act was extended to June 30, 1973 the Senate voted for it grudgingly. Some national leaders have expressed themselves in favor of a volunteer army to replace the draft but a large segment of public opinion feels that such a volunteer army would become a military elite. On the other hand, some say that the poor and disadvantaged would be the only volunteers—due to the high scale of pay in this "mercenary army." To which the usual response has been that the poor and disadvantaged would be unable, health-wise and education-wise, to measure up to the high standards required of volunteers.

The Military Selective Service Act asserts that all men of draft age must register for the draft. This must be done within thirty days before or after the young applicant reaches his eighteenth birthday. Sometimes the draft board is lenient with those who register a few days late but it is wise to register on time. One who fails to register may be in for trouble. He may be given the option of being arrested or of joining the armed services immediately.

A short time after registration, the local board will mail the registrant a certificate which he should keep with him at all times. After a few weeks, perhaps he will receive a Classification Certificate which he should fill out completely and mail back to the local board within ten days. It should be filled out carefully as it may have a bearing on the classification that the registrant will eventually be given. He should be sure to keep a record, either carbon or Xerox, of all completed forms and other papers he sends to the draft board.

It is impossible, of course, in this brief chapter to cover all the details of required procedures. For even the draft boards themselves vary in their procedures. The prudent course is to get in touch with a draft counsellor as soon as possible, even before the applicant's eighteenth birthday. Usually draft counsellors, like doctors and lawyers, differ in their level of competence and personal attraction so it is advisable to find one in whom the applicant can repose his personal confidence. They have no official connection with Selective Service. (See the listing of agencies that might offer useful help in regard to local counsellors or special problems at the end of this book.)

There is a vast amount of literature about the draft that might be useful to the draftee but it should be kept in mind that a particular book or brochure might become obsolete when revisions are made in the draft law from time to time. (See the Bibliography at the end of this book.)

The most difficult question confronting many applicants is whether or not to apply for conscientious objector status. Some men undergo a profound mental anguish in making this decision. It is a decision that may have great immediate impact on the man himself, his family and friends, and may reverberate through all the remaining years of his life. Those who have made the decision pro or con have discovered that the inner conflict has affected their whole psychological attitude toward themselves and the world. Many young men, having made the decision, have suddenly come to realize their responsibility to the world about them. Sometimes this awakening of consciousness has prompted them to take part in violent demonstrations which may have been imprudent but their motivation was to make a dent in public opinion, even at the cost of endangering their lives. Perhaps for the first time in their lives they experienced a felt sense of the need of spiritual integrity. They became the persons God intended them to be. Adults have sometimes felt uneasy about the brash courage with which the younger generation has subjected old customs and sacred cows to sharp scrutiny. To a large degree, this unsparing honesty has emerged from the younger generation's anguish over the draft.

Conscientious Objection

Conscientious objection is as American as apple pie. The Continental Congress in 1775 first proclaimed the immunity for those whose religious principles forbade them to bear arms, at the same time urging conscientious objectors to contribute services to their country consistent with their religious principles. Under the present Act, deferments are no longer given automatically to all college students but a young man who conscientiously objects to bearing arms can be granted exemption from military service. He can apply for 1-A-O classification. If this is granted, he may be assigned to non-combatant duties, such as medical service. One who objects to any service connected with the military should ask for a 1-O classification. He may be ordered to serve two years in some civilian work "contributing to the maintenance of the national health, safety and interest." To obtain either classification, the applicant must prove that his objection is based on "religious training and belief" and that he is sincerely opposed to "participation in war in any form."

The term "religious training and belief" is very broad. The U.S. Supreme Court has ruled that you do not need to be a member of a church or even believe in a Supreme Being in order to show that your objection to war is based on "religious training and belief." All that is necessary is that the personal religion you live by causes you to oppose participation in war. Letters from relatives and friends attesting to your opposition to war would be helpful in proving your point to the draft board. Another U.S. Supreme Court decision (1970) said that the law exempts from military service "all those whose consciences, spurred by deeply held moral, ethical or religious beliefs would give them no rest or peace if they allowed themselves to become a part of an instrument of war." However, it should be noted that the belief must be ethical, moral or religious, not merely a political view.

As a result of these decisions, it is quite clear that your objection must be religious and must be sincere. Some members of the draft board may suspect you are motivated by cowardice rather than by religious belief. They cannot, however, reject an application for CO status arbitrarily: they must base their adverse judgment of you on facts in your draft file. This is why it is wise to have in your draft file letters from friends or relatives or copies of remarks you have published or made in public before you applied for CO status. It is not necessary to prove you are sincerely opposed to all kinds of violence. All that the draft board can demand is proof that you presently object to participation in all wars.

This is the major hurdle for Catholic applicants

for CO status: this requisite that they oppose participation in all wars. The draft board generally knows that most Catholics are not total pacifists, not opposed to all wars, and that most of them, in accordance with the Just War theory, hold that a just war is at least theoretically possible. Therefore, they cannot obtain CO status. Why? Because the U.S. Supreme Court in an 8-1 decision (March 8, 1971) ruled out the possibility of selective conscientious objection. Justice Thurgood Marshall, who wrote the majority opinion, said that only those who object to all wars can be granted CO status. He claimed that if selective conscientious objection were allowed there would be so many COs that the government's right to raise and support armies would be hampered. Secondly, he said that selective conscientious objection is generally based on political considerations, not moral and ethical beliefs.

So we find many Catholics (and Protestants) barred from becoming COs, official protests from Catholic and Protestant groups to the contrary notwithstanding. Most of the Americans who avoided the draft by going to Canada during the Vietnam war were selective conscientious objectors who were not opposed to all wars but only to the Vietnam war. As a result of the Supreme Court decision, a conscientious Catholic sincerely convinced that a particular war is unjust is confronted by three choices: he can choose to violate his conscience by consenting to induction into the armed forces; he can go to jail; he can leave the country. What his conscience forbids, his country commands. To disobey the law in this case is not disloyal. He is loyal to a higher power than the state.

Justice Douglas dissented from the majority opinion in the above-mentioned case. He said, "Conscience is repudiated. . . . the Court has done violence to the basic philosophy of the First Amendment and we take a step backward." I heartily agree. The decision does violence to conscience and to the First Amendment.

The decision runs counter to the thinking of the American Bishops in their 1968 Pastoral Letter entitled "Human Life in Our Day." In this Pastoral they urged that laws make provision for all selective conscientious objectors: "We therefore recommend a modification of the Selective Service Act making it possible, although not easy, for so-called selective conscientious objectors to refuse—without fear of imprisonment or loss of citizenship—to serve in wars they consider unjust or in branches of service (e.g. the strategic nuclear forces) which would subject them to the performance of actions contrary to deeply-held convictions about indiscriminate killing" (*Human Life In Our Day*, p. 70).

In this Pastoral Letter the American Bishops spoke in praise of COs generally, remarking that it is not at all surprising that some intemperate criticism of war as an instrument of national policy should be found among youths. "The burden of killing and dying falls principally on them" (p. 68). The Bishops admitted that COs are sometimes suspected of cowardice, conceding that individual cases of cowardice do occur among them, as in all tests of heroism. But they said that such a blanket charge would be unfair to selective COs. "A blanket charge of this kind would be unfair to those young people who are clearly willing to suffer social ostracism and even prison terms because of their opposition to a particular war. One must conclude that for many of our youthful protesters, the motives spring honestly from a principled opposition to a given war as pointless or immoral" (p. 68).

Amnesty

What about the question of amnesty? Should the American government grant pardon to, and release from all penalties, those young men who evaded military service or deserted from the armed forces? There were 70,000 young Americans who left the country during the Vietnam war in order to avoid the draft: there were probably 40,000 deserters as well. Amnesty after wars or rebellions has often been granted in American history. George Washington gave amnesty to men who took part in the "Whiskey Rebellion" and Jefferson, Lincoln and Grant made amnesty proclamations. President Truman pardoned 1,500 men who evaded the draft in World War II.

Many church leaders and political luminaries endorsed amnesty proposals while the Vietnam war was still in process. Churchmen in certain cases felt that they had placed young men in the cruel dilemma of obeying conscience or the law and were somewhat responsible for their plight. Religious condemnations of the war had generated resistance to the war and so it is understandable that some clergy should view amnesty in a favorable light. The Interreligious Conference on Amnesty, with participation by Catholics, Protestants and Jews, issued a statement (March 28, 1970) in which they made clear their consensus that amnesty be granted to draft resisters and deserters with no strings attached.

Many national leaders have come out in favor of amnesty. Senator George McGovern, campaigning for the Democratic nomination for President in 1972, said that if he were elected, he would support amnesty for both draft evaders and deserters and even supported amnesty for those who planned the war! Senator Robert Taft has made a strong plea for amnesty but feels that deserters do not merit it because they violated their oath. On the other hand, some deserters say that they left the country because they did not want to become criminals in an immoral and illegal war. Their position is that the government which bears guilt for the war has no business passing judgment on them.

The central theme underlying the controversy over amnesty is the need for reconciliation. After a war, the first thing necessary for any nation is to pull itself together by healing the divisions left in the wake of the war. It is not always easy to read God's mind but it does seem to me that God would want us to reconcile and forgive those presently estranged from us as a result of the war. Forgiveness does not seem to be the right word. In fact, many deserters do not feel that they have committed a crime or sin, and millions of Americans are asking, "Who are the real culprits behind this tragic war"?

Prosecution of all resisters and deserters, (about 115,000), would be a task of monumental proportions. At first glance, it might seem that resisters could be freed from prosecution while deserters should not be released. But many supporters of amnesty claim this would be a sort of class discrimination. Evaders and resisters were generally from the college-educated middle class while deserters were usually disadvantaged and less-educated servicemen who found themselves caught in the draft before they really understood their situation.

At any rate it does seem to me good sense to grant amnesty to all "irregulars" after the Vietnam war. By refraining from punishing them, we do no dishonor to the war dead but demonstrate a humane compassion for resisters and exiles that will help restore our country to health and sanity. Amnesty will bring the country together by giving our "irregular" young men who opposed "involuntary servitude" an opportunity to become productive citizens. I think most of us would agree with Kenneth Zwicker of Keene, New Hampshire, father of a deserter who went to Sweden. "It would be an awful waste to put him in jail. He imposed on himself an exile of three and a half years. He's a sensitive and talented person who's been through a lot. It would be a shame to lock him up and not have the benefit of his talent and energy and experience in the world outside" (N.Y. Times, December 27, 1971, p. 22).

One fact is obvious: the large-scale dissension, restlessness and fragmentation that ferment in America at the present time. The country is in grave need of reconciliation of all its divisions. Until there is reconciliation, the wounds we have sustained during the Vietnam war, both in Vietnam and at home, will never heal. And while we are about the work of reconciliation let us not forget those men who paid the heaviest price, the 50,000 military dead and the other thousands of veterans who will have to bear their wounds with them to the grave.

BIBLIOGRAPHY

WAR

Bainton, Roland, *Christian Attitudes Toward War and Peace,* Abingdon, 1960 (paper).

Clergy and Laymen Concerned, Editors. *In the Name of America,* Turnpike, 1968 (deals with war crimes).

Fall, Bernard, *The Two Vietnams: A Political and Military Analysis,* Praeger, 1965.

Hersh, Seymour, *Chemical and Biological Warfare: America's Hidden Arsenal,* Bobbs Merrill, 1968.

Hormann, Karl, *Peace and Modern War in the Judgment of the Church,* Newman, 1966.

Long, Edward LeRoy Jr., *War and Conscience in America,* Westminster, 1968.

McSorley, Richard, *Kill For Peace?,* Corpus, 1970.

Quigley, Thomas (editor), *American Catholics and Vietnam,* Eerdmans, 1968.

Swomley, John, *The Military Establishment,* Beacon, 1964.

———, *Amnesty: The Record and the Need* (study guide), Clergy and Laymen Concerned.

Taylor, Telford, *Nuremberg and Vietnam: an American Tragedy,* Quadrangle, 1970.

Zahn, Gordon, *War, Conscience and Dissent,* Hawthorn, 1967.

THE DRAFT

Hodges, Graham, *Draft Information Packet* (contains brochures and books on the Draft for pastors), Hodges Publications, Watertown, New York (Box 293).

Killmer, Richard and Lutz, Charles, *The Draft and the Rest of Your Life,* Augsburg, 1972.

Tatum, Arlo and Tuchinsky, Joseph, *Guide to the Draft,* 3d edition, Beacon, 1970 (contains lists of local counsellors and counselling services in the various states, also addresses of Selective Service directors and birthday and lottery numbers).

Tatum, Arlo (editor), *Handbook for Conscientious Objectors,* revised periodically, CCCO, 2016 Walnut Street, Philadelphia, Pa. 19103. CCCO also publishes *News Notes* five times yearly to cover changes in the Draft, etc.

DRAFT INFORMATION AGENCIES

CCCO/An Agency for Military and Draft Counselling, 2016 Walnut Street, Philadelphia, Pa. 19103 (has many regional offices).

American Friends Service Committee, 160 N. 15th Street, Philadelphia, Pa. (has many regional offices).

Interfaith Committee on Draft Information, Room 830, Witherspoon Building, Philadelphia, Pa. 19107 (resources for draft information for high schools).

National Interreligious Service Board for Conscientious Objectors, 550 Washington Building, 15th Street & N.Y. Avenue, NW, Washington, D.C. 20005.

National Draft Counseling Directory (a listing of draft counselling centers in the U.S. with addresses, published by Youth Counseling Foundation, 711 S. Dearborn St., Chicago, Ill. 60605).